Praise for
Tech Humanist

There are countless people that claim to know where the future will take us with technology, but that is all worthless without knowing what impact it will have. Kate is not only the best person I know to guide us, but this book is the practical crystal ball for it. Most experts scare us into listening to them with tales of a tech Armageddon, while Kate actually gives a damn about humans and tells the truth. She is the true Tech Humanist.

— *Scott Stratten, Hall of Fame keynote speaker, President of UnMarketing Inc, and bestselling author of 5 business books including UnBranding, UnSelling, UnMarketing, The Book of Business Awesome (and UnAwesome)*

Data and technology are changing society — for good or ill. Kate O'Neill shares a powerful vision that will enable us to leverage these disruptive forces for the benefit of humanity.

—*Dorie Clark, adjunct professor at Duke University's Fuqua School of Business and author, Entrepreneurial You and Stand Out*

Given the pervasiveness of technology of every corner of our lives and its profound impact on us, it stands to reason that the best way to improve humanity is to improve our technology. Kate O'Neill has been a leading voice in the movement of better align business with the human experience, and Tech Humanist serves as a clarion call for business leaders to recognize the power they have in crafting a better tomorrow. We can only be future-ready if we are human-first. As O'Neill succinctly puts it, "the future of humanity depends not on benevolent robots but on benevolent businesses." Her timely book is the wake-up call that we all need right now."

— *David Ryan Polgar, founder of All Tech Is Human & co-host of Funny as Tech*

If you're a business leader navigating technological change, the way to truly and radically disrupt your industry, is to inject a whole lot of humanity into the technological investments decisions you're making. Kate O'Neill's Tech Humanist is your roadmap to doing just that.

— *J. Kelly Hoey, Author, Build Your Dream Network*

❂ ❂ ❂

A stirring examination of a very modern fork in the road: technology at all costs, or technology in service to us all? Read the thoughtful and timely Tech Humanist... before it's too late.

— *Jay Baer, Founder, Convince & Convert, Hall of Fame keynote speaker & emcee, and best-selling author of 6 books*

The future is not a problem for tomorrow; today, while we still can, we must master our rapidly changing technology to shape the best future for humanity and our businesses. Kate O'Neill shows what's happening and what's at stake, and lights the paths forward. There is no better guide.

— *Jeffrey Zeldman, author, Designing With Web Standards, co-founder of the multi-city web design conference An Event Apart, and founder of studio.zeldman, a digital design studio in New York*

In 2003, I helped launch the Web Analytics Association. In the early days of the association we debated the definition, and scope of "data analytics."

Two of us on the board argued for a broader definition. We had a glimpse into where the collection and use of this data was heading. In 2012, the association changed its name to the Digital Analytics Association. They revised the scope and mission to the broader definition we shared earlier in our history. I don't share this to boast that I was right. I share this to give you a glimpse how our decisions today either limit or expand our possibilities.

We are living in a time of transformation whose pace far exceeds any that humanity has seen. Think about all the changes that the industrial revolution brought into this world. Think back to 2003 when there was no Facebook, no Twitter, no drones, no iPhones, no autonomous vehicles, etc. Our technological growth is impacting more people today, far quicker than any technology from the industrial revolution ever did. So how will we be prepared to handle this change?

Kate O'Neill's "Tech Humanist" should be your guide to navigating our digital future.

— *Bryan Eisenberg, Partner Buyer Legends and New York Times best selling author*

I love technology. I love people more. As our world becomes ever-more digital, the question of where we – as a people – belong in work is at play. In Tech Humanist, Kate O'Neill does an amazing job of pulling it all together. Back in the early 2000s, I used to say that everything is 'with' not 'instead of.' Without humanity technology will not evolve. Without technology humanity will not evolve. Tech Humanist makes the case for this duality and the magic that happens as it all comes together.

— *Mitch Joel, Founder, Six Pixels Group. Author, Six Pixels of Separation & CTRL ALT Delete*

The future of technology is human. Our ability to bring the human experience to ever more sophisticated tools will be what separates success from failure. Kate deftly weaves together both the roadmap and the toolkit to help us humans understand how to make the most of it.

— *Robert Rose, Founder and Chief Strategy Officer of The Content Advisory, author of Killing Marketing and Experiences: The 7th Era Of Marketing*

For the past two decades, the Computer History Museum has chronicled the amazing rise of the technology which just in our lifetime has become the most powerful agent of change the world has ever known. While the stories of creativity, invention, innovation, and impact are fascinating, what all this means for the future and humanity is what we are poised to take on now as an institution. And nowhere has this become more clear to me and my colleagues here at the museum than in reading Kate O'Neill's blog post entitled "The Tech Humanist Manifesto." The idea that we need to develop and embed in all future technologies the very best of ourselves and our ethics and ultimately have the goal of those emerging technologies to make us better humans has resonated deeply into our own plans of what we will present, discuss, and debate going forward.

After reading the manifesto, my initial thoughts were "Kate should write a book on this." Which I am very happy that she has done, and now her humor, excellent insights, and heartfelt philosophy can reach the leaders and influencers throughout the world. And the rest of us too.

— *Gary Matsushita, Vice President, Computer History Museum*

Tech Humanist

How You Can
Make Technology
Better for Business
and Better for Humans

By Kate O'Neill

Acknowledgements

Thank you to everyone who has helped me research, has engaged in endless discussions about technology, humanity, and the future, and has put up with my obsessing over the topics.

Big thanks to the cover designer Denisa Anamaria Badoi for designing such a wonderful cover.

Huge thanks to my editor, Jocelyn Bailey, for her keen eye, the insights she contributed, and her positivity.

And an enormous thank you to Robbie Quinn, my photographer and now my husband, whose work I use on the back cover and "About the Author" page, who helps make the future more meaningful for me.

Dedication

To the brave women and men of the #MeToo movement, for the honesty and courage that will ultimately help create the best futures for the most people.

A note on my use of the generic gender-neutral singular pronoun "they"

Throughout this book, as I describe scenarios involving unspecified actors, instead of the arbitrary use of a single gendered pronoun in generic use, whether "he" or "she," instead of the clunky "he/she" or wordy "he or she," and instead of painstakingly alternating between the uses of gendered pronouns, I have adopted the use of the singular "they." It was the American Dialect Society's 2015 word of the year, and it reflects a trend toward more inclusive language. Just like the spread of technology into all aspects of life, you'll get used to it.

***

"We live in a society exquisitely dependent on science and technology, in which hardly anyone knows anything about science and technology."

— *Carl Sagan,*
"Why We Need To Understand Science" in The Skeptical Inquirer Vol. 14, Issue 3 (Spring 1990)

CHAPTER 17

The Future You Create

WE NEED TO TALK ABOUT the future.

Because we're hurtling toward a version of it that many of us feel uneasy about, and it doesn't offer the vast majority of us the options we need for the quality of life we want and deserve. And because we still have the chance to make it better.

But the actions we need to take and the decisions we need to make to ensure a better future are often prevented by how abstract the consequences of those decisions can seem. It is one of the more bizarre attributes of human consciousness that the future can indeed seem so far off and even frightening when we are, in a sense, living in the future. This moment that you're in, as you read these words: this very moment was a future from a past already a moment ago. In other words, the future of the past is now. (It's a bit trippy, isn't it?) Whatever you did in the moments preceding this one had some role in determining what you would be doing in the future, as in: what you are doing right now. For example, at some point in the recent past, you decided to read, and you opened this book (or e-book or audiobook). Now those decisions are behind you, and a future full of ideas lies ahead of you.

Yet what the future holds confounds and even paralyzes people. In surveys about their greatest fears, people often cite climate change, cyberterrorism, and people they love dying[1]. (Not public speaking, contrary to popular myth.) Those fears all have in common that they point toward an unknown future. People share a lack of clarity about where we'll be, what we'll be doing, and how the world will look around us.

A great source of anxiety for many is how rapidly and radically the world seems to be changing or about to change because of technology as a whole, including the implications of data, automation, and artificial intelligence. It's challenging even for experts and pundits to keep up with the technology that exists and is created every day, and how any of it stands to change the way we live: our work, our day-to-day living, communication, shopping, entertainment, relationships, transportation, healthcare — everything.

And, of course, we worry about how the future stands to change our businesses. It's true that what has changed around us in the last few decades is potentially dwarfed by what lies ahead of us. In fact, 70–80 percent of CEOs say that the next three years are more critical than the past fifty years[2]. Even the world's top business and institutional leaders are not immune to worrying about what the future brings. Indeed, perhaps leaders especially suffer from anxiety about the future because they feel such a heavy responsibility to make decisions without knowing the road ahead. Maybe you're a leader who feels this way. Maybe you're a leader who struggles to make sense of the technology landscape, yet you must steer your company and decide where to invest and how to adapt. Maybe you're not what you would call a leader, but you still want a clearer picture of the path to the future so you can do your own work more effectively.

Here's what I want to offer you: To me, the idea that the future is never fixed or certain is actually encouraging. Truly, it fills me with hope. I think of the future largely as something we continuously alter, shape, or at least influence with what we do today.

That thought also fills me with a sense of duty because it means there are always many possible futures that depend on me and you and everyone else doing our parts in the whole. It means our everyday actions have more power to shape outcomes than we are often comfortable admitting. And it means we can't afford to be intellectually lazy as we consider the scope and scale of technologies that stand to change lives and cultures all over the world, some for the better, some not so much. But who makes that judgment, and on what standard?

Whatever your beliefs about destiny versus free will in any sort of spiritual sense, when it comes to business strategy, it's wisest to exert whatever influence you have over the outcome of events. If you can adjust your strategy ever so slightly, align your team's mindset, optimize your resources, maximize your impact, and in so doing, ensure you have the best possible shot at thriving in the future, why wouldn't you do it? Would you still fear the future if you knew you'd done all you could to create the best future possible?

> ## Would you still fear the future if you knew you'd done all you could to create the best future possible?

If dealing with the best possible future is about making the best decisions, how do you make them? How do you even begin?

The future is uncertain, but so are the impacts on the future from today's decisions.

At any rate, the future isn't just one unknowable thing. It stretches out ahead of us in a range, from the very nearly graspable next second, to the minutes ahead we can likely predict with great accuracy, to all of tomorrow's meetings and plans, to the dreams of next year, through the rest of our lives, and beyond. Certainly those moments just ahead of us are more predictable than whatever will happen decades from now. But as a leader, you must be able to think about the immediate *and* the distant future, and to make decisions that answer to both. The pressing needs of this moment and now this one and now this one are all about urgency and responsiveness.

But you can't live in that emergent state. You can't lead from there, and you definitely can't innovate there. To lead and to innovate, you must pull back from the insistent demands of the present and allow your mind to take in some of the wider time horizon. Allow yourself to notice the trends of the marketplace, the way people are buying now, the way people talk and communicate, the way they spend time.

Of course, in addition to foreseeable change, the future will inevitably bring sudden change, loss, tragedy, and disappointment: in other words, events over which you have no control. Our day-to-day decisions guide the future, but they do not govern it.

Innovations will always come along that may benefit society at large, or add convenience or enjoyment to people's lives, but cost a sector of companies their consumer relevance. Inventions, shifts in taste, and cultural trends are bound to render whole markets obsolete. We will deal with those changes as they come. Sometimes, if you have cultivated the right kind of resourcefulness and agility in your organization, you can adapt and survive. We will explore what that requires, because that kind of foundational uncertainty goes hand in hand with what the deference we tend to show to "technological progress," and, if you are a leader, that kind of adaptive survival is what you presumably want for your organization. But the factors you can't control and the companies that will fail are not the focus of this book; instead, we will look at how to maximize the impact of the influence you do have, and how to make your mark on society and history with the best and most relevant version of what you offer.

The biggest problem with the future, though, is that it *feels* like something we can deal with tomorrow, not today.

We may recognize a pattern that could become a problem—tightening cash flow, a thickening waistline, warming global temperatures—but find it far easier and more pleasant to think instead about the latest social media trend, the show we've been binge-watching, or simply the more concrete, immediate problems demanding our attention right this second. We may find tomorrow's problems too conceptual or too undefined, and we may be tempted into magical thinking that problems will somehow be solved on their own or by others—rather than that they may scale into bigger problems. It's both too easy to ignore the nagging challenges the future is already showing us and too easy to accept as inevitable the inequities that are likely to grow with it.

The tomorrow that is now today doesn't always look like we thought it would. Just because our surroundings don't look like something straight out of *The Jetsons* doesn't mean the changes around us haven't transformed human life—for better or worse. For all the flying cars we *don't* have, think of all the connectedness and access to knowledge that we *do*. After all, Wikipedia is in many ways more transformative than jetpacks. And beyond documented knowledge, think of the connected services. The net value for humanity of much of the app-driven service economy may be debatable, and the inequality it fosters may even be harmful; but the mere fact that rides, laundry, food delivery, massages, house cleaning, and other services are available with a few taps is still kind of an amazing development.

Now it's up to us to make sure we harness all that amazing potential and use it to make the future less frightening and more hopeful for everyone. To do so, we must make intentional choices that align the best of technology's promise, and the business objectives that provide fuel to it, with the best and broadest of human objectives.

Being a Tech Humanist means recognizing that we encode ourselves into machines; that what we automate will scale; that we need to be aware of what we encode and scale. We'll explore all that further, but for now, Tech Humanists see that the future of humanity depends less on robots being subservient to us or dumber than us and more on how robots and other automation are deployed to service business goals. Most of all, we know the future depends on aligning business incentives and human needs, as it is predominantly business that ramps up automation and machine-driven experiences in the interest of efficiencies and growth.

In other words, Tech Humanists know the future of humanity depends not on benevolent robots but on benevolent businesses.

The future of humanity depends not on benevolent robots but on benevolent businesses.

Trends and predictions are not merely the vague indulgences of "futurist" provocateurs, no matter how exciting or terrifying their viewpoints may seem. Because rather than outsource the visibility of the road ahead to prognosticators, Tech Humanists need to develop those skills for themselves. In a rapidly-changing landscape, this is how all of us must learn to live. One eye on the now, one eye looking into the distant future. Making the most of the moment; ready to adapt to survive.

This is why true "success" in digital transformation—the Tech Humanist way—must look beyond the immediate results to the sustainability of the solutions, as well as beyond the company's own profit motives to the future as a whole and the betterment of human experience and quality of life, impact on the planet, and so on. To the best futures, in fact, for the most people.

About This Book

Many books about digital transformation already exist: books on transformation strategy, on the coming automation renaissance, on technology selection and deployment, on operational excellence, and so on. But the most grounding and clarifying emphasis of all is rarely explored: What about *us*? What does the evolution of human experience look like in the context of an increasingly machine-driven future? How can business leaders navigate their technology investment decisions with a willingness to be part of making better futures for more humans?

I firmly believe humans need a better future, and business is the channel through which the biggest impacts are ever likely to be made. So I have written this book hoping to reach leaders and aspiring leaders who are motivated to bring about positive change in their own organizations as well as for as many people as possible whose lives they touch.

In this book, I would like to provide you with the tools to lead with a mindset of strategic hope, treating the decisions you make now as if the future depends on it—because it does. Some of this book, then, will explore the nature of technology's relationship to business and to human beings. Some of it will revisit business leadership fundamentals in the context of what may seem like radically new ideas about data, digital tools, and emerging technologies.

This book offers a new way of taking stock of it all, a fresh way of thinking about it. An integrative, holistic framework will give you a clear point of reference you can always come back to if you get lost.

It may seem, at times, a bit too idealistic, or perhaps even naïve. I assure you I have no delusions about the capacity of humanity for wrongdoing. I am well aware, for example, of the mess that US politics have increasingly become, and even global politics. But because of these messes, now is especially the time for a simultaneously optimistic and pragmatic view on how to achieve the best futures. Without a strategy, I fear we'll simply spiral.

As I was writing *Pixels and Place* in 2016, it became increasingly clear to me how interrelated the data landscape was becoming with what most of us think of as "real life": our concrete physical surroundings, seemingly so unmalleable, so unmovable, but in actuality deeply mingled and dependent on insights from the data generated by our movements, by our interactions, by our transactions.

So while in *Pixels and Place* I wrote about designing for the connected landscape across the dimensions of physical surroundings and digital data, I began to see the imperative of laying out a framework and toolbox for designing the entire set of human experiences that will increasingly be driven by data and technology, and making decisions about investing in it.

Then I spent time speaking about connected experiences, digital data trails, and so on, and I found my writing and speaking topics becoming broader, harder to pinpoint: technology and its impact on humanity, how data and algorithms are shaping our landscapes, how automation is changing the future of human work, etc. I've spoken about automation and the future of business operations and gamification strategy. I've written about chatbots, about the impact of automation and emerging tech on financial services, about the future of retail, about smart cities, and more.

Something has been pulling at me across all these different topics. Perhaps you feel it too: the somehow-connectedness of what people tend to discuss separately as topics like digital transformation, automation, disruption, digitization, artificial intelligence, connected devices, smart cities, and so on. The common thread was data—and not just any data, but personal data, combined with the emerging use of technology in increasingly ubiquitous ways.

It was time to write another book. There was just too much to write about not to. And it would have *something* to do with the impact of data and technology on human experience.

In pondering how to narrow that down, in pondering what coherent focus my work truly has, I have considered the full scope of the changing business and consumer technology landscape. I have considered data privacy, the ethics of data collection, the importance of data equity, and the social justice implications of algorithms. I have considered blockchain, both in terms of cryptocurrency and its non-currency applications, and what it might mean for the future of human experience. A futurist perspective, I guess.

So, right then: back to the future. Well, with a side trip to the recent past.

Sometime in mid-2017, I sat down and wrote a manifesto (as one does on a Friday). It was about data and technology and automation and artificial intelligence and self-driving cars and the Internet of Things and wearables and everything that is converging to make human life nearly inseparable from technological progress.

It was also about the fact that we—humans, that is—create this technology, and we embed our values and biases into the logic and decision-making of what we build. So it's increasingly important, I wrote, that because technology is what we encode of ourselves, we must encode the best of ourselves, which means we must *become* the best versions of ourselves.

And in that manifesto, I declared myself to be a "tech humanist."

That declaration resonated, apparently. Thousands of people read and shared the blog post, many of them commenting and emailing me to tell me how important they felt this perspective was.

I do think it's important. I think it's a movement.

In one form or another, what I've been writing and speaking about is "tech humanism." And the Tech Humanist approach is nothing short of an attempt to make the world better by making technology better—better for business *and* better for humans.

The Tech Humanist approach is an attempt to make the world better by making technology better—better for business *and* better for humans.

So herewith, I'd like to invite you to consider that you are a Tech Humanist too, or that perhaps you should be. As you read and consider whether you are indeed a Tech Humanist, I want you to feel that the title of this book refers not to me, but to you. Because it does.

Tech humanism is a movement we need. It's an idea whose time has not only come, but whose time is long overdue.

When I published *Pixels and Place* in 2016 about the integration of physical and digital experiences, automation was already a small part of the story—in that many of the experiences are reactive, responsive, adapting to human movement, involvement, behavior; providing different experiences based on location, movement, etc.

But since that time, automation and artificial intelligence have taken up a considerable amount of business and public attention, surfacing new challenges of the impact of technology on human experiences and on humanity as a whole. Those challenges include what automation means for human jobs, what AI means to our human future, and other concerns of an almost existential nature. Those broader topics are taken as part of the landscape of this discussion and are touched on here, but the real focus of this book is the alignment of business objectives and human objectives with the technology-driven experiences created by business; those that collect and use personal data, those that adapt and scale and shape culture.

A Guide to Creating the Best Futures for the Most People

The Tech Humanist mindset is about aligning your business goals with broader human goals so that the more you succeed, the more you bring humanity with you. It is, in part, a methodology for digital transformation—which is about making your organization more data-informed, scalable, and future-ready—that doesn't lose sight of the human experience. It's intended to help you navigate rapidly changing landscapes by making sense of your strategy *as it relates to people*, aligning your organization, which is *your people*, collecting the right data relating to *the people you serve*, deploying the right technology *to interact with people*, and ultimately investing at every meaningful stage in the experience had by the people who do business with you.

Like any strategy shaped by the Tech Humanist approach, this book serves several aligned and integrated purposes: to guide business to greater profit through automation, to guide the public to greater awareness of the data collection and transactions that undergird their daily movements and interactions, and fundamentally, to lay out a roadmap for a future with more clarity, more transparency, more opportunity, and more moments of…let's call it "ambient human happiness." And with that, fewer experiences of confusion, distress, and anxiety.

I want this book to inspire you and energize you, but also to provide you with practical, adoptable takeaways. I'm offering a framework: a set of philosophies and ideas about culture that can be adopted individually or organizationally.

And it's a rallying cry that I hope you will join me in amplifying: That our future should be brighter because of technology, not scarier because of it. That our opportunities should broader because of technology, not limited by it.

This book will explore how we become the best versions of ourselves to create the best version of the future.

How we evaluate the biases we encode into machine logic and decision-making and reduce the risk of scaling absurd experiences.

How we review our decisions for unnoticed privilege and how we reduce exclusion and risk to others who use our products, who are tracked and targeted by the data-collection systems we set up.

And how we develop diverse and inclusive teams so that our work has the best chance of being representative, and of not causing harm.

It's about encoding technology with the best of our humanity to empower business with tools to scale the right kinds of values. At its heart, this book is about creating the best futures for the most people.

At its heart, this book is about creating the best futures for the most people.

"The best futures for the most people" is open to some

interpretation. It could mean the absolute best futures, which would mean a whole series of things would have to go exactly right and yield a perfect outcome that results in the most people having the very best future possible. And in this same absolutist way, "the most people," by definition, is everyone. So one way to think of it is that the goal is for everyone to get to live out their very best future.

Clearly that's a little ambitious. Meanwhile, there's also the interpretation that we're talking about the "best futures" achievable given the various limitations of context and reality. And that this should be true for the most people possible, given the circumstances.

Whereas the first interpretation was overly ambitious, this interpretation is a little defeatist. And it alleviates pressure on people who are in positions of power and privilege to help those who are living on the margins. Within the topics that are part of this book's scope, *the margins* refers to people working in sweatshop conditions to create computer parts and accessories; the people working long, difficult hours in warehouses for massive online retail operations; the people whose region's natural resources are plundered for silicon components; and so on. We who enjoy relative comfort need to feel some pressure to improve the human experience for these people, too.

So the most sensible take on "the best futures for the most people" is a hybrid of these interpretations: We need to work to make the improvements that are feasible now, and we need to keep the ideal in mind as a benchmark we may never reach but should always strive toward.

There's no good reason why technology can't be used at scale to improve the lives of every living person in the world. Achieve that outcome requires that it be a priority, though, and it likely requires that it be a priority that aligns with business goals.

The point is: The best way to deal with the changes brought about by emerging tech is to make human experience more meaningful.

The best way to deal with the changes brought about by emerging tech brings is to make human experience more meaningful.

❋ ❋ ❋

With algorithms, automation, AI, big data, and other emerging technologies, we will see business achieve scale like never before.

We have not always approached business strategy and growth with the necessary rigor and discipline, and we can't afford to be sloppy when the results can scale so rapidly and impact human lives so thoroughly.

We need to build the meaningful future we'll *all* need.

After all, automation, AI, and other emerging technologies are accelerating and gaining traction largely because of their usefulness in achieving business outcomes. So what we need more of is a robust discussion of these considerations from the standpoint of humanity, experience, and meaning. Once you integrate these viewpoints and align your efforts to a business-driven, tech-enabled model that results in better experiences and better futures for the most people, you become a Tech Humanist.

And I feel, more than ever, that we have an obligation to the future. For ourselves, the generations after us, and—without hysteria or hyperbole—the planet as a whole.

Who Is This Written For?

I'll be totally honest: My primary motivation for the work I've done leading up to and including this book is to improve the world for as many people as possible in the best way I can. And the best way I have determined to affect the most people's lives is by helping business leaders recognize the power and potential of improving human experience on a massive scale.

So perhaps you, too, are a business leader. A CEO, a head of a business unit, perhaps marketing, technology, operations—any of these.

As a speaker for and advisor to large corporate clients, cultural institutions, associations, cities, and organizations, I have focused more and more over the past few years on helping leaders understand how to take a human-centric approach to digital transformation. I've had the opportunity to speak to executive audiences at hundreds of events about data and emerging technology, and to meet and talk with thousands of leaders in roles across technology, marketing, operations, and beyond, from companies large and small across every industry imaginable. In practice, this means I've spoken with thousands of leaders—many like you—and the consensus is they feel mounting pressure to decide where to invest on emerging technologies like augmented reality, beacons, blockchain, the Internet of Things, and so on.

Perhaps you are reading this because you are struggling to articulate and execute a strategy that aligns your company's organizational purpose with the momentum of emerging technology and societal trends. I have written this book to help prepare leaders like yourself to navigate near-constant change, manage evolving expectations, innovate relentlessly, build actionable understanding of the market at internet pace and scale, automate where it makes sense to do so, and achieve sustainable growth and results—all while creating a more meaningful and memorable experience for the human on the other side of the transaction.

I also recognize and respect the considerable groundswells around socially-minded programs that do "tech for good," "AI for good," "data for good," and so on. I'll touch on those here and there, but because I believe business objectives determine so much of human experience, my emphasis is largely on the business cases for technology, data, automation, and AI, and how to make those consistent with positive human outcomes. Since businesses are wired to succeed one way or the other, my goal is to help them find human-centric paths to success.

In writing this book, I am thinking of three major groupings of audiences:

1. Leaders of corporations and cultural institutions, from CEOs to executive directors of museums, civic leaders, and so on: those who directly guide the strategic future of entities responsible for a wide chunk of human experiences.

    •   CEOs: anyone thinking about transformation, growth,

and scale

- CTOs: anyone building a tech or IT organization, making staff decisions and considering a tech organization's evolving model

In this audience are people who are:

- looking at the landscape and trying to decide where their resources should go
- struggling to understand how to adapt and prioritize in a chaotic world
- in a position to make technology better for business and better for humans.

For you especially, I have included the methodology I use in my executive workshops, as well as the Human-Centric Digital Transformation canvas I've created to help leaders make sense of organizational change in the context of digital transformation.

Perhaps you're not currently a senior leader. Perhaps you're an aspiring executive, and you see the challenges in the adoption of technology within business. I hope this book will provide you with insights, frameworks, and the vocabulary to step more confidently into a leadership role prepared to make a better future.

2. Practitioners: interactive designers, strategists, developers, user experience professionals, product managers, and so on: those who directly create the experiences humans have. You may already be working on navigating these changes for a company. Or you could be in any of these roles and merely have an interest in the future and want to see it grow to be healthy for humans. Perhaps you work in an operational role. In fact, you should find value in this book if you work across any of these roles:

- Product people: anyone thinking about the product development roadmap from a holistic human-centric perspective
- Operations people: anyone building and optimizing the organization, evaluating automation, and managing overall operations from a human-centric perspective

3. And finally: humans. Of all professional backgrounds, all social standings, all cultural affiliations, rich and poor, powerful and marginalized, young and old. We all—the human in any context—have something to gain from considering the ideas in this book and understanding a bit more about how business is using personal data to create more customized, dimensional experiences. We can all learn how to be smarter users of products and consumers of goods and services.

Whether you are a business leader or not, a practitioner or not, know this: I am writing to you human-to-human, with empathy for the dilemmas you face and with bright hope for your future—just as I have hope for the bright futures of everyone else in the world.

There's one thing I hope we all have in common: Most of the people who will read this book already suspect that we can make technology better and make human experiences better.

If you're here and you doubt that this is possible, or if you're a leader who simply wants to profit off of the manipulation and misery of others, I will not be not writing to convince you. But I do welcome you to read this book and see if any of my ideas resonate.

I'll try to keep the rah-rah high-mindedness to a minimum, but it's in my nature to look at things as systems, to see everything in an integrated, interconnected way, and to seek the best outcome for everyone. And what I see when I look at this moment in time is that we've got to figure out ways to dimensionalize meaning throughout every kind of experience *before* and while we amplify them through automation.

I want to give you practical guidance, no matter who you are, on how to achieve the best possible results from the integration of tech, business, and humanity so that we all have the best chance of a bright future.

How to Use This Book

※ ※ ※

By all means, I invite you to read this book from start to finish. I've written it with that intent, but I understand, despite your desire for a better future, the messy reality of the insistent now and the many pressing demands on your time. So I've also structured this book to be digested in sections, taken chapter by chapter, and even read a few pages (or screens) at a time.

It's also my hope that you will read it as a team, as an organization. The approach is meant to be cross-disciplinary, so it should have as much relevance to a marketing leader as to a technology leader, an operations leader, or any aspiring leader. Or for that matter, any human.

It was tempting to break the book into several conceptual parts, like "for business" and "for humans," or "how to make human life better" and "how not to make human life worse." Or even to write separate books. But as you'll see, a great deal of the underlying message in how we actually go about making technology, as the subtitle promises, better for business *and* better for humans is through integration. Thus, the viewpoints on business and human experience are woven together in each chapter, labeled for an actionable takeaway.

In Chapter 18 - What Makes Humans Human, we begin by establishing some understanding of what our most defining characteristics are, what it means to make technology better for humans, what the scale of data and technology solutions means for humans, and how machines, rather than threaten to replace us or dominate us, can be used to amplify what is best about humanity.

Then we get right into the actionable.

Chapter 19 - Human-Centric Digital Transformation presents a framework for getting your organization future-ready, human-centric, and aligned.

In Chapter 20 - Get Clear on Purpose, we look at the principles that allow you to develop your brand and culture so that you can design meaningful experiences at scale.

With Chapter 21 - Integrate we look at the macro idea that integration is an important and recurring theme—the integration, of course, of technology and humanity and of business objectives and human objectives, but also at other trends that reveal the same overarching force of integration.

In Chapter 22 - Make Experience Meaningful, we dig deeper into the design of human experiences and how to make them memorable, differentiated, and meaningful.

It can be tough to think about something as abstract as meaning being compatible with something as concrete as measurement, so in Chapter 23 - Measuring the Unmeasurable: Strategy and Data Modeling for Meaningful Experiences we look at some approaches to thinking about modeling meaningful interactions, modeling the business in data, and directional indications that you are on the right track.

Chapter 24 - Upgrade the Whole System: Digital Transformation, Purpose, Alignment, Future-Readiness explores various opportunities to make technology better for business without losing sight of the human perspective: a look at what digital transformation truly means, a human-centric model for digital transformation, experience strategy, and meaningful growth and scale.

In Chapter 25 - Iterate as You Learn, we explore the benefits of designing experiences through incremental improvements so there's less pressure to get it right the first time and less resistance to making changes now rather than later, when they're "perfect." I also introduce a new methodology for Automated Integrated Human Experience Design.

Chapter 26 - Adapt: Navigating Change and Growing Meaningfully is about taking what you learn and stepping up your game, while Chapter 27 - Evolve: Ready Your Business for the Future helps you think through reaching the next level for your business.

By this point, it should be clear that big changes are coming and how they'll affect us all, and you may be ready to change your own business. But how can we be confident our transformations will create the best futures for the most people? In Chapter 28 - Ethics at Scale, we explore the wider implications of the machine-driven experiences of the future, as well as the ethical considerations of many of these technologies and platforms so that our decisions and investments are sound.

Chapter 29 - Design for Meaning explores a range of approaches to creating interactions, transactions, and other experiences that reinforce the dimensions of the relationship you want to emphasize.

Because the future of human experiences are so likely to be driven by automated systems, Chapter 30 - A "Tech Humanist" Approach to Machine-Led Human Experiences offers considerations to make them as meaningful as possible.

Once you have gained a deeper understanding of what could be meaningful within the experiences you create, you can begin to plan how to Chapter 31 - Scale for Meaningful Experiences.

You'll notice that the section on technology, Deploy Relevant Technology, is nearly the last section, which may seem odd for, y'know, a book about technology. But this ordering underscores the value of thinking about strategic purpose and the other considerations laid out earlier in this book as an input to deciding what technology to deploy and how. It is also intended to be a companion to an interactive playbook full of ideas to prompt and inspire you and your colleagues to devise implementable solutions for your business and to consider how those solutions will impact the humans who use your products and services. The full complement to the playbook is available at techhumanistbook.com.

The final part, the epilogue, is both a review and a forward look at the principles and philosophies that will carry us into the future with a grounded view of humanity—the mindset to make the decisions that empower the best possible future for you and for all of us.

CHAPTER 18

What Makes Humans Human

IF WE'RE GOING TO TALK about the impact of technology on humanity, we need to explore the state of emerging technology in its many forms. Even more urgently, we need to get on the same page about humanity.

When intellectuals in the past considered the human condition, they were often weighing our experiences in contrast to the gods; for example, Alexander Pope's "to err is human; to forgive, divine." Maybe part of the difficulty in objectively evaluating our place in the context of human versus machine is that when we ask ourselves these sorts of questions, we are conditioned to see the other party as all-powerful, omniscient, and immortal. And we are used to casting ourselves as helpless, subservient, flawed creatures at the mercy and whim of the divine. When I hear people describe their anxieties about the rise of the robots, I can't help but feel they're projecting the attributes of Greek mythology's gods onto tech. Not that a robot-driven dystopia isn't possible, but being burdened by an irrational fear of it doesn't help us actively prepare for the better future we could have.

If we detach from the comparisons both to the digital *and* the divine, what is left when we consider what it means to be human? What makes humans *human*?

That's a question I often ask people in workshops and keynotes.

I've heard hundreds of answers. If you did the same—if you were to survey, say, a hundred people on the street and ask them what really makes humans *human*, what characteristics really define humanity— the answers you'd receive would likely relate to creativity, empathy, or love. Chances are, most of the survey answers would also fall into two broad categories:

1. Creativity, imagination, problem-solving, innovation
2. Empathy, compassion, love

Those are admirable qualities of humanity, no doubt. They are very relatable and endearing traits that are part of what make humans what they are. They are amplifiers of universal human values.

I don't know, however, that we could say they are unique to humans. Nonhuman animals have been observed to share some of those qualities. For example, otters solve the problem of opening shellfish by cracking them on rocks, and elephants are demonstrably affectionate with each other. What's more, I don't know that machines couldn't approximate some of those traits, or at least be perceived to. Crudely perhaps for now, but eventually in a way that will probably cause us some existential angst.

Perhaps what's more unique is a sense of value, of intuition, of alignment, of our affinity for companionship. Perhaps none of these is particularly unique to us, at least as they concern other animals. Perhaps these senses won't even be unique to us relative to machine-based intelligences for very long. Perhaps it isn't critical that we have qualities that are truly unique from nonhuman animals or machines. But that doesn't mean the question isn't worth considering, because there are tremendous opportunities for maximizing the best of our human potential.

For me, the most distinctive human quality is this: Humans crave meaning.

The most distinctive human quality is this: Humans crave meaning.

We thrive on meaning. We seek it, we create it for ourselves, we hold vast and complicated systems of beliefs to support it, and when it is offered to us, we tend to find it irresistible.

I'm talking about meaning at every level, from semantics and communication to the most macro sense, at an existential and even cosmic level. The popular notion that story is a key element to achieving memorable interactions with people in business and branding points back to the need for a framework, for an explanation, for a takeaway.

We create the meaning we crave through shared understanding, alignment, relevance, and doing what matters.

Some readers will ask here, is it really human nature to seek meaning, to create equity? Isn't it more our nature to compete, to conserve energy by being lazy, or to seek status, hierarchy, or position?

Fair question. There are always the good and bad of human nature, the angel and the devil on our shoulders. We are not driven merely by animal survival instincts; we have higher consciousness. And we can extrapolate and project likely consequences: We can anticipate the results of our actions and amend our decisions accordingly. The more sophisticated our technologies become, the more sophisticated we must become. The more we demand of technology, the more we must encode it with the best version of ourselves, and the more we must *become* the best version of ourselves.

Where we sometimes struggle is to do this at scale. We need to be reminded why it matters to make decisions that work at scale — globally and historically. Across space and time.

The Value and Potential of Humanity

"Any sufficiently advanced technology is indistinguishable from magic."
— Arthur C. Clarke's third law, from "Hazards of Prophecy: The Failure of Imagination"[5]

A few times a year, when my family gathers for birthdays and other celebrations and I'm not able to be with them in person, they call me via Skype or FaceTime. My husband and I join the party virtually as they pass us around and pan the room, and for a while we're all but transported to the loving chaos of the scene. Despite how many video calls and chats I've experienced in my years working in and around technology (hint: there have been *many*), those calls still feel magical to me.

They feel especially magical when I think about video chat's long path from imagination to ubiquity. Although people imagined the possibility of videotelephony as early as the 1870s, the actual technology needed to create even a primitive form of video call took nearly half a century to develop. Many iterations followed, but Skype, which has become the brand synonymous with the technology of video chat and conferencing, didn't launch as a company until 2003. Those years between the 1900s and the early 2000s included many incremental inventions critical to the success of what is now a fairly common tool and platform, but most people didn't experience video calls until they became commonplace closer to 2010.

Whenever I can see and talk with my growing great nephew and niece from nearly eight hundred miles away, I'm struck by this as an example where technology has truly enriched our lives.

Much of what is written about the future is dystopian. Science fiction tends toward the cautionary.

But there's a nondystopian way to see the future. A vision where technology and culture accentuate the best of humanity and scale resources for more people.

In a sense, it is a vision of using technology to achieve humanity writ large.

It's not all like this, of course. Plenty of the devices, gadgets, apps, services, and tools developed and sold into widespread usage would be harder to romanticize.

You know how when we're kids, our parents told us we weren't living up to our potential? (Oh, that isn't everyone?)

Well, maybe it's kind of like that with humanity.

Just as we tell children to "live up to their potential," perhaps we should view the opportunity for humanity this way. What we design and build has the potential to amplify certain characteristics, whether ultimately beneficial or harmful to ourselves. And perhaps the opportunity we have with AI, with automation, with technology at scale is to make decisions now that help humanity live up to that potential and scale in a way that's good for us.

Are there things about the human experience, about human intelligence, that we have misunderstood and underestimated?

What is the best of humanity? Have we been held back by not being challenged enough? If humanity is really taken to scale, or brought to scale, what does that look like? We have so much rich potential to live fulfilled lives, to create beauty, to serve each other's needs, to foster deep senses of community and support, to enjoy meaningful experiences of all kinds.

So the question is: *Can* we use artificial intelligence as a point of human improvement?

Many people have been reacting to climate change and artificial intelligence in similar ways—with hand-wringing, cultural concern, but not much evident behavioral change.

I'm convinced we're at a moment of awakening for humanity. Artificial intelligence and climate change are two of the megatrends poised to cause massive, ongoing waves of unprecedented, exponential transformation. Both have destructive potential, but both also seem to be beckoning for human ingenuity and dedication to steer us in positive directions.

Perhaps people don't know what to do, exactly. Maybe they're doing small things, such as recycling every day, but they sense that the small things seem so inconsequential compared to the enormity of the problem. We know that it will take solutions at scale, but we don't feel empowered to create them.

In a similar way, you could tell people to learn to code, but they know we're a long way past IBM Watson's win on Jeopardy in 2011[4]. Maybe they can sense that knowing how to get "hello world" on screen won't stop robots from taking over their jobs.

Am I saying that robots will take over people's jobs? Well, yes, in a sense. Automation is a rising tide, with waves that keep sweeping and sweeping over the tasks we do at work, smoothing the tasks and jobs over like rocks in the surf, with the emergence of each technology trend, making processes more efficient and reducing the need for manual intervention. So yes, for all jobs, there's a point at which it makes more sense to have machines perform the task. But that point varies from job to job, and new human jobs will form along the shoreline, too.

What does that mean for the humans whose jobs have eroded into sand? If we ever get to a point where humans can learn to breathe underwater, we'll be able to let the majority of people have their needs met by systems of machines that address basic resources and needs. And the fact that we generally become more tech-dependent year after year suggests we're learning how to breathe underwater. But the economy and social structures aren't there yet to support what life looks like without jobs, so we scurry to the shoreline and keep trying to adapt to the new levels.

But part of what limits us is the discrepancy between business goals and human goals.

Business is an abstraction that, fundamentally, allows humans to centralize resources around solving a problem in pursuit of providing a product or service. It's about teamwork. It's about a common purpose. The efficiency that comes with teamwork and common purpose is one of the benefits of this structure, but efficiency isn't the goal. Yet profit, which is a measure of economic efficiency, is commonly held as the highest standard of success for business. It is indeed a measure of proportional decision-making over the long term, of business health, of preparedness for sustainability; but it is not in and of itself sustainability, health, or justification for all decision-making.

The shortsighted pursuit of profit is damaging. Profit is a ratio, and it's only one way to gauge the success of a company.

A more aligned way to look at business goals—a way that aligns with human goals—has to do with how relevant its offering is to the people it serves and how successfully it helps those people achieve their goals.

The acceleration of technological development is largely driven by business goals.

So if we want human experiences to be more meaningful and to live up to humanity's potential, we have to create greater alignment between tech goals—i.e., business goals—and human goals.

If these goals could be more in alignment, if they could find some room for agreement, there'd be so much potential to improve the lives and living conditions of so many people. Capitalist opportunities with consideration for human impact: That's the power of thinking integratively.

There's something, too, about the power of human scale when it's assisted and accelerated by technology. Think of Kickstarter and the rest of the crowdfunding category: The premise is just humans helping humans achieve, but the platform itself organizes and legitimizes the effort to collect money. Or think of the Patreon model and platforms like it, where fans can support the creative work of writers, artists, and other creators whose efforts are buoyed by their monthly patronage. (Patreon hit a hitch, though, when they tried to pass overhead costs on to subscribers. It cost them the loyalty of some of their creators and supporters before they reversed the decision.)

At the same time, the very existence and common usage of these platforms highlights the existence of systemic problems. GoFundMe is often used to collect donations to support someone who needs emergency surgery or has sudden medical expenses due to an accident. In fact, almost half of the funds raised on GoFundMe between 2010 and 2016 — $930 million out of $2 billion — were for health-related campaigns.[5] GoFundMe even has informational resources on their website about medical crowdfunding since it has become so common.[6] In short, the platform's success is a very telling indicator of how insufficient healthcare coverage is, particularly within the United States.

But the fact that people in emergency situations now have a platforms like GoFundMe also points to massive opportunities for humans to help humans in other ways. When humans organize, they have tremendous capacity for compassion and support, and technology potentially empowers humans to organize to unprecedented degrees.

The Tech Humanist opportunity for companies is two-fold: either facilitate this intentionally, or get out of the way.

❀ ❀ ❀

A humanistic philosophy starts with the simple agreement that humanity is important. That's it. It's not a political agenda, economic plan, or religious affiliation; it's just the idea that somehow human life is valuable and worth respecting.

If you will go with me a step further, it's the sense that we all have an ethical responsibility to maintain, if not improve upon, a baseline quality of life for all human beings.

From there, we look at technology and data and the impact of digital life on everyone. How have smartphones changed our lives? How has the internet changed the world?

GPS has forever changed the experience of exploring a new city.

Voice assistants are a boon to the blind.

Online communities have been a great resource for people who are otherwise isolated.

There is a lot to be hopeful for, a lot to appreciate. And there are benefits and drawbacks to everything, including technological progress. What matters is context, and how lives are impacted by innovation.

We do need to know that living in a culture with an ever-accelerating sense of time might mean that we have to resist an ever-narrowing horizon, and that we lose our sense of greater perspective in the FOMO frenzy; that believing our experiences aren't real unless we share them and receive a few (or preferably many) likes might cost us our peace of mind.

We need to recognize the humanity in the data we mine for profit; to see that most of the time, analytics are people. We need to realize that everything we do in the world creates a data trail, and that who we project ourselves to be — that self, that digital self — is our aspirational self, liking things and connecting with people and wandering through the digital world in awe. And as our aspirational self, our digital self deserves due privacy and protection in every way.

So much of the way we've derived our identity and sense of accomplishment, achievement, and contribution is subject to radical overhaul in the next decade and beyond. More jobs will be automated, augmented, enhanced, and yes, eliminated. And certainly new jobs will be created—but we can't wait for them. We have to begin reimagining what meaningful contribution could look like.

We need to reimagine our lives around new ideas of meaning: What relationships look like when they're conducted across physical distances but connected by intimate virtual space; what communities look like when they're multifaceted network nodes, and not just in houses of worship and town squares; and what "what we do for a living" means as jobs shift, as our understanding of contribution changes,

The future of work is unknown. The future of human meaning that has traditionally been derived from work is also unknown. We don't know where we're going to substitute the next level of experience.

We need to consider what it means to be human when the characteristics we think of as uniquely ours can be done by machines. What, then, will be the value of humanity?

It will take a renewed, committed focus on humanity, which in practice means creating integrated, meaningful, relevant experiences. But it also means looking at the issues that immediately surround this topic: data trails, personal privacy, undue influence of algorithmic content, the increasing scope and cultural threat of filter bubbles, and the polarization of society.

Could we deprogram the inequality in social systems through focused efforts in data science and technology, and eventually counteract the systemic effects of racism, sexism, all the isms?

We need to level up *everything*; become better people in a better society, surrounded by better machines with better encoding.

And it needs to happen in concert and in harmony with a mindset toward creating more meaningful human experiences at scale.

Where purpose as a tool of clarity and alignment on the business side aligns with purpose as a dimension of meaning on the human experience side.

Where integrated strategy aligns with integrated experiences.

Where digital transformation, which is fundamentally about business agility with business data, which is fundamentally about people, aligns with the understanding that analytics are people, and that relevance is a form of respect, but so is discretion.

Where the resolve not to be blind to absurdity and not to let absurdity scale aligns with the recognition that meaning and absurdity sit in constant tension with each other, and that where a lack of meaning exists, it opens up a void into which absurdity can flow.

Where priority, goals, and alignment complement clarity, resonance, and meaning.

* * *

Technology is endlessly fascinating. But I'm even more fascinated by humans and our endless complexity. Humans are such complicated systems of nerves and emotions and thoughts and impulses. What I always find most interesting are people; and people are the ones who make technology, who use it, who benefit from it.

People are not inherently interesting because they use technology. Our tools are not the objects of my primary interest. After all, ravens use tools. So why am I not, say, a tech ravenist?

Well, unless we find out about other intelligent species with technology in the universe, humans are the best identifiable link between the dominant technology and the rest of organic life on this planet and beyond.

So our best hope for integrating the needs of all living things and all technological progress is in our own enlightenment.

We need technological progress. It will bring us cures for disease, intergalactic travel, safe and efficient energy, and new forms of communication, among so much else.

But we need to wrap that progress around human advancement.

And we need our own enlightenment.

We need a more sophisticated relationship with meaning and with meaningfulness, at every level: in communication and in pattern recognition, at an existential level.

We need to want the best futures for the most people.

And it's not that I'm a human exceptionalist, exactly. I've been vegan for twenty years, after all, which I point out to illustrate that I don't think rights are something only humans deserve.

If I'm around when machines become sentient, I'll probably care about AI rights.

So it's not that I think humans are so special that we deserve protecting and coddling, except that just maybe we are, and just maybe we do.

Whatever humanity is, it's worth advocating for.

Whatever combination of fascination and flaws it was that

produced Shakespeare, Gloria Steinem, Paris, pizza, the Brooklyn Bridge, beer, Nelson Mandela, denim, Mary Tyler Moore, coffee, chocolate chip ice cream…

I don't know if any of that is really the best of humanity. To some extent, I don't think it matters what the "best" of humanity has been up until this point, because the future demands that we work to become our true best now. Somehow striving for it, making something that lasts, and striving to make the best future for the most people — that may well be what the best of humanity is.

In any case, the Tech Humanist in us all must recognize that the opportunity *does* exist to invent life-changing tools that enrich and improve us, make us smarter, deepen our connection to each other, and strengthen what it means to be human: our senses, our awareness, a yearning for meaning, our connection to each other, our connection to what matters.

Integrating Meaning and Machines

John Henry said to his captain,
"A man is nothing but a man,
But before I let your steam drill beat me down,
I'd die with a hammer in my hand, Lord, Lord,
  I'd die with a hammer in my hand."
— "John Henry," folk song, anonymous[7]

Folk stories pitting "man against machine" go way back. People through history and across cultures have seen hard work as a virtue and have tended to derive a significant sense of accomplishment from their output, from their sense of contribution, and from earning a place in their community through their labor.

So it stands to reason that when people think about robots and automation, they get anxious about being replaced and worry about what replacement will mean for their future. They have massive, immediate, obvious economic concerns, and it remains to be seen whether Universal Basic Income or some other model of providing for people's needs will work best. But even aside from the issues of individual earnings, people tend to see machines as an existential threat.

But even to whatever extent those concerns are founded, our humanity is not best served when it's defined or assured by asserting superiority over machines. Engines, mechanical devices, and computers have long surpassed human capabilities, with rare and legendary exceptions, in strength and endurance, speed and complexity of calculations, and far beyond; and sophisticated automation and artificial intelligence will continue to surpass our abilities. So if our humanity is wrapped up in being better at certain tasks or functions, then with time and technological progress we will no longer understand our humanity.

Instead, our humanity—our understanding of humanity, and any attempt to model it and amplify it through machines—should be grounded in what grounds us, which is meaning: a sense of purpose, an emphasis on what matters, and the drive to create and enjoy more meaningful experiences.

Imagine a world where you are served and provided for by seamlessly integrated technology that seems to anticipate your needs and fulfill them according to your preferences, with no cause for concern about your privacy, your safety, your opportunities, or your financial state. This simplistic utopian description isn't far from describing the *opposite* in nearly every way of the current state of technology as it scales through automation. The difference between these extremes of utopia and dystopia has to do with whether or not human needs are kept in focus.

The relationship between humans and machines has always been interesting to observe. Every innovation seems to spark fear.

One of the most dissonant moments in pop culture that I can recall was a scene in the movie *The Matrix* when the main character is learning new skills and one of his human colleagues remarks, "He's a machine!"

Perhaps it's not a coincidence that when many people think about immigrants, they think about them taking up resources, committing crimes, and deflecting funds from programs that "should" be for native-born citizens.

When people who have disproportionate privilege think about

marginalized people of any sort achieving equality with them, they think with fear: They think about encroachment.

Yet time and time again we've seen that when we seek integration, we find increased opportunities.

But it takes thinking about a model where every human being is important, where no one is any more entitled to resources than anyone else.

A scarcity model won't serve us well. We need to work toward abundance. Leave room for resources to become scarce and for us to adapt in that event, but evolve toward models that expand the economy, expand opportunities for everyone—and when I say everyone, I'm including the sophisticated robotic intelligences of the future. Why shouldn't they have opportunities when that becomes relevant, too?

We use the word *autonomy* when we talk about self-driving cars, which should prompt us to take a step back and ask whose autonomy we're describing. In everything we automate, we should be seeking a form of freedom and autonomy enabled or empowered by technology that truly lifts humanity, versus having our freedoms and opportunities hampered by technology. At times we will do best to approach automation as an augmentation of our human capabilities, and at other times automation will serve us best as a replacement. Having a framework that allows for either as needed with little existential angst will allow us the greatest freedoms in the long run.

As business looks toward digital transformation, the foundational question becomes: Do you automate models as they exist, knowing they may be limited? Knowing, for example, that there may be flaws in how your business model could perpetuate or even exacerbate inequality at scale? Knowing that certain kinds of digital behavior are addictive and toxic? You can't simply sit back and wait for new and better models of human behavior to emerge. You have to build for the future with a certain amount of consciousness of the present and flexibility for evolution, knowing that new patterns may emerge as human culture adjusts to being surrounded by immersive, intelligent, automated technology.

So I'm not saying we shouldn't be cautious about robots and automation. But rather than treat the subject with abject fear, we should be devising means to ensure our safe evolution into a species that coexists with sophisticated robots. Which means we should ensure that robots and other machines are programmed to maximize mutual benefits. Which means we need to understand what truly benefits us most, at our core.

We should ensure that technology is designed to amplify what we find to be most meaningful because the inverse would result in a world full of meaninglessness. A world full of absurdity. It's absurd, for example, when we're asked to confirm our humanity by clicking a reCAPTCHA checkbox that says "I am not a robot." (That absurdity is turned nicely on its head when we see the viral video of the robotic arm holding a stylus that clicks a laptop trackpad and satisfies the crude requirement of the test.)

How do we know, practically speaking, what meaningful human experiences are? We'll need to examine meaning and define experiences, and we'll need a methodology for designing them. That's included here.

Everything we experience with our senses and our intellect would count, but we also know that many of these interactions and transactions are created and designed for us by companies for a commercial purpose. What's more, these commercially driven experiences for humans are increasingly administered by machines.

One key question is: To what extent do they intersect with our intrinsic desires for meaning and fulfillment, and how much better *could* they?

I think most would agree that a future built to amplify meaningful experiences is preferable to a future built to amplify meaningless experiences. But how do we get there? That's what this book will help demonstrate.

Amplifying Meaning in Business and Life

I think a lot about absurdity because I think a lot about meaning, and they're related, in a way. They're locked in a constant state of tension in the world, and in life in general. Meaning is a purposeful structure or awareness, and absurdity is a contrast between things as they are and things as they make sense to us.

Wherever a lack of meaning, or a lack of intentional effort to define meaning, exists, a void of sorts opens up. And into that void, absurdity can flow. It can flourish and scale and take over our time and attention, dragging us down into its lack of clarity and focus.

Wherever a lack of meaning exists, a void opens up into which absurdity can flow.

So it is our opportunity in this world to push back on the encroachment of absurdity by creating more meaning. Any kind of meaning, in any of its variations: alignment, mindfulness, intention, fulfillment, contentment, resilience, and so on. The more intentional we are in our efforts, the more we state what we are trying to do and what is important to us, the more we keep absurd experiences at bay.

It's true at any level, from the purely personal to corporate strategy. Meaning helps us understand what's important. Meaning is what matters. Meaning should be determining our priorities and focus, and it should shape our goals and experiences. We each have a different understanding of what is meaningful because we have different values, different backgrounds, and different priorities.

At some level the universal objective of all life is survival and propagation, but as humans, that is only one layer of the meaning life offers. We are capable of conscious pondering of a higher meaning, and the very fact that we ponder meaning at all suggests that we may do best in a framework that recognizes meaningfulness.

Once we acknowledge that meaning is important to us, then we are left with an ethical imperative: to help others achieve their meaning, or at least not to hinder each other from achieving meaning.

Yet we live day to day in routines that obscure meaning. We work, many of us, in jobs devoid of meaning, and those jobs eat up huge chunks of our waking lives.

So if that's true, we need to re-evaluate our systems of work and education. We need to revisit our economic underpinnings, which assume that more equals better, when in fact more meaningful equals better, and more doesn't always mean more meaningful.

Unfortunately, it's also easy to lose sight of what is meaningful to us in business or in life. And when we lose that grounding, we make decisions that move us further away from what matters to us. Business is full of absurdity because we're moving fast and most businesses don't create a culture that reinforces what matters at a human level. So we end up doing and saying absurd things. We follow processes that make no sense, we use language to describe things that no one outside our workplace would understand, and so on. It's hard to step back from our surroundings and take inventory of opportunities to call out the absurdity and make the things we do more meaningful.

But the moment you find yourself thinking, *I'm not sure this makes sense*, that's a really big clue. Because making things make sense is what meaning does.

The influence of meaning takes different shapes. In marketing, it's empathy—an ability to relate to the perspective, context, and needs of the person you're serving, and to serve up relevant content and experiences. In art, the work becomes more meaningful the more it reveals great truths.

In business, the shape meaning takes is strategic purpose. When it's articulated, it guides every decision. Being clear about meaning in business by understanding your strategic, organizational purpose leads to better focus, better prioritization, more clarity of direction, etc., which ultimately facilitates growth, scale, and profit—all while setting the right context for creating more meaningful experiences for customers. Such alignment between organizational purpose and customer experiences allows a leader to discern what fits along the path and what is a distraction. That clarity is especially important in the context of data-driven opportunities, emerging technology, and all manner of digital transformation demands.

> In business, the shape meaning takes is strategic purpose.

So with an open mind and the right tools, you can step back, examine what is truly meaningful, and reduce the absurdity in your brand, culture, and operations, and in the use of data and technology to create experiences.

We need to be clear that what has changed around us in the last few decades is potentially small potatoes compared to the changes that lie ahead of us. As I mentioned earlier, two-thirds of CEOs surveyed by the advisory firm KPMG in 2016 said that the next three years would be more critical for their company than the past fifty years. In addition, only sixty of the companies that were in the Fortune 500 in 1955 were still there in 2017. (Meaning, fewer than 12 percent of the Fortune 500 companies included in 1955 were still on the list sixty-two years later in 2017, and 88 percent of the companies from 1955 had either gone bankrupt, merged with or were acquired by another firm, or still existed but by total revenues were no longer in the top 500.) In other words, business models that lasted more than a hundred years just aren't competitive or relevant anymore.

And yet, in some ways the world around us really *isn't* changing that much or that fast. Maybe it just feels that way because we're consumed with our own difficulty in adjusting to it. After all, whatever you're doing right now is normal, and there are parts of today's normal that would have seemed weird just ten years ago. But a significant portion of what you're doing today looks just like it looked a decade or two ago. Fundamentals don't often change. We connect with each other at human scale and human speed. The kinds of experiences that align with our universal human nature feel timeless no matter what, whereas the experiences that are driven by the technology trend of the moment feel as though they are constantly changing. See The Shape Versus the Nature of Experiences for more about that difference and how to think about it relative to your business offering.

So we need to do both of these things:

1.   Accelerate change in business and reduce the time to market of anything that makes business more adaptable and successful

2.   while *also* making technology and business processes more aligned with human motivations and behaviors and needs.

These things need not feel as though they're fundamentally at odds with one another.

We need to reimagine business around new ideas of value, and to understand what value means when it's about an integrated you in an integrated world. The economic might of business accelerated by exponential technology is too volatile to leave unexamined for its effects on societal health, for its philosophical merits, for the good it *could* do if its broadest objectives aligned more closely with those of humanity overall.

Still, change is change. Whether it happens on a corporate level or a human level, any kind of change comes with tension or excitement. Organizational change brings about many of the same anxieties people feel when they experience personal change. You have to manage the people inside the company: the personalities and human reactions. And often the best way to know how to go about doing that is through the clarifying power of organizational purpose. We know this because humans crave meaning, and as we'll talk about throughout this book, purpose is the shape meaning takes in business.

For a while we talked about better tech in terms of usability. That was the heuristic, the high-water mark for success in terms of tech that complemented human need. But things have gotten rather more complicated. With the introduction of more and more forms of automation, with the emergence of data-driven experiences, with the growth of artificial intelligence, with the advent of augmented reality and the maturing of virtual reality and the hybridization of mixed reality, and with the flourishing of wearable technologies, we have reached a new level of need for mutual benefit in terms of what drives technological advances for business and what drives technological progress for humanity.

There will be a new class of perceived errors, where usability means something new in the context of artificially intelligent systems, conversational interaction, and GUI-less interfaces. Or perhaps it doesn't mean something new, but it requires new levels of thoughtfulness to achieve.

We need, in other words, an expansive and widely adopted philosophy of technological humanism, or tech humanism for short. And those who espouse this philosophy must be committed to creating the best futures for the most people.

Humans and the Meaning of Work

"I am, somehow, less interested in the weight and convolutions of Einstein's brain than in the near certainty that people of equal talent have lived and died in cotton fields and sweatshops."
— *Stephen Jay Gould*[8]

We've already discussed how important meaning is to humans. And one of the major sources of meaning for us is our work.

Work has long been integral to our sense of identity. We've literally defined ourselves by our jobs! An awful lot of people have names that are based on the jobs their ancestors had, like Butcher and Baker and Tanner and Carpenter and Brewer and Judge and Weaver, etc., etc., and this happens in other languages too, all over the world. It's a universal human instinct.

We derive a tremendous amount of meaning from our work — the sense of accomplishment, of problems solved, of having provided for ourselves and for our families, of having made a contribution, of having value and self-worth.

The reason why this question matters so much is best captured in the results from three studies. One is a widely cited study done at the University of Oxford in 2013. It found that 47 percent of US jobs were at risk of being replaced by automation over the next two decades. [9]

A subsequent study in 2017 building on the earlier research found that jobs in certain sectors were at far greater risk of being automatable: as much as 80 percent of transportation, warehousing, and logistics jobs, for example. [10]

A third study done by the OECD, an intergovernmental group whose membership consists of mostly well-off countries, took a closer look at job skills and which of those might most easily be replaced by automation. The upshot is equally bracing: Across thirty-two countries, 14 percent of jobs were considered "highly automatable" (in other words, with a probability of over 70 percent); and an additional 32 percent of jobs "have a risk of between 50 and 70% pointing to the possibility of significant change in the way these jobs are carried out as a result of automation."[11]

There are enormous business advantages to automation and even potentially tremendous human advantages, but while we acknowledge that, let's not pretend there aren't significant socioeconomic impacts that follow massive waves of job automation.

And let's also be sure we're not overlooking the psychological impact: the displacement of human workers, the disruption of work-derived identity.

Increasingly "entry level" and "low skilled" jobs will be replaced or displaced, augmented or eliminated entirely by automated process and machines. Across most studies, the types of jobs typically cited as most likely to be impacted include cashiers, factory workers, truck drivers, call center staff, and some kinds of healthcare workers.

Also, we can expect, particularly in the US, a disproportionate effect on people of color and on immigrant populations. Spencer Overton, president of the Joint Center for Political and Economic Studies, noted that 27 percent of black workers are heavily concentrated in thirty job types that are at high risk of displacement or replacement due to automation[12], including cashiers, truck drivers, and other jobs types consistently cited in these types of studies.

As if that weren't enough to make us careful about how we proceed, there's massive digitization of the human work experience: fundamental shifts due to digitization in employment; data and digital models that have enabled the gig economy; and of course the data and algorithms that are used more and more often throughout the talent management process, from sourcing to hiring to managing and so on.

Moreover, it's yet to become clear what the impact will be to the job scope of doctors and radiologists in situations where machine learning systems can offer faster and more accurate diagnoses, and to the job scope of legal researchers from natural language processing capabilities that can search and aggregate potentially relevant material far more quickly and thoroughly than humans. While those jobs may not rapidly be replaced, the composition of the work will change; demand for those services from humans will decrease; and the need for people skilled in interacting with the machines may increase. But to what extent and in what proportion remains to be seen.

Not only is there an ethical imperative to understand this, but also an economic imperative: The implications of the widespread replacement of human labor and displacement of human earnings potential are still unclear. Universal Basic Income experiments are underway in closed markets, but how will they scale?

Economists, sociologists, policy-makers, etc., need to be studying the potential impacts.

And we know with automation the answer to this dilemma is not going to be "work harder" or even "work smarter." The reality is, there potentially comes a point at which the majority of jobs may not be fulfilled by humans.

That future is still unknown.

In the meantime, as Tech Humanists, what do we do to make the most of this transition?

We have to recognize the possibility of a post-human-work world, or at least a world where human work has fundamentally changed—so that as we look at automation, we see the impact on both the experiences automation creates and the experiences automation displaces. Because in the future scenario where all the human work has vanished, where do humans get the same sense of meaning? That meaning we have historically derived from work will have to come from something other than work. We need a better answer.

The Tech Humanist proposal is to ensure that business objectives and human objectives are as aligned as possible so that as automated experiences scale, they scale human values with them, and a sense of what is meaningful to humans surrounds us. This is one reason why it's imperative that we figure out how to reconcile business objectives and human objectives and make them make sense together.

Because businesses won't be successful long-term without scaling through digitization and automation.

But humanity won't be successful long-term without meaning.

Humans Add Value by Being Human

In the near term, as humans learn to coexist with machines in the work world, there will be a heavy emphasis for human work on emotional intelligence. Understanding nuance is where humans play the most valuable part in this process.

We understand patterns, to a point—but machines are even better at patterns. Machines are excellent at pattern detection and recognition but may or may not have the programming needed to recognize what is meaningful about a pattern.

Someone trained a machine to parse *Where's Waldo?* images using Google's facial recognition service, and it spotted Waldo in 4.5 seconds.[13] What's *your* personal best? Mine's not nearly that fast.

Obviously the machine's capability exceeds similar human capability, but we could interpret this as an augmentation to human capability. As a species, you could say we are now better at finding Waldo. After all, humans developed the technology; now it is available to augment our limitations and expand our opportunities.

But certainly we can expect job shifts and the creation of new roles. After all, since the introduction of ATMs in the US, human bank teller employment has grown steadily by 2 percent each year[14]. The composition and scope of tasks that comprised the work a human teller would do before and after ATMs has changed, but the need for the human remains. That's not a guarantee that there won't be dramatic shakeups in some areas of human employment, but it's a testament to the human ability to adapt.

What's more, I would like to give humans credit. Time and time again, throughout history, we have devised new and clever ways to create value and have invented new roles for ourselves. My favorite people are always the ones who have been through a few personal reinventions; as a collective species, we have that power writ large. I have no reason to believe we won't reinvent ourselves again in some fashion.

In the meantime, we can "re-purpose" and "up-purpose" human workers into higher value and more meaning-centric roles. Humans and machines together can detect patterns quickly and interpret them, layer meaning and nuance on top of them, and so on.

An integrated approach may include having people:

- Respond to cues that suggest need for human intervention
- Respond to emotional cues

- Respond to sensory cues
- Respect context and meaning
- Recognize bias and encode our best selves into our machines

The approach to adding human value to human experience is the basis of Human-Centric Digital Transformation, which we'll explore next.

CHAPTER 19

Human-Centric Digital Transformation

IF YOU ARE LEADING A company or in any way involved in navigating decisions about the future on behalf of an organization, you have likely run up against the dilemma of what technologies to embrace, where to invest, how and what to accelerate within the organization, and what to prioritize.

I am happy to introduce you to my Human-Centric Digital Transformation model, with which I have advised numerous companies to strategize and plan their transformation efforts. We'll get more into the how and why of digital transformation in Digital Transformation is Bigger Than "Digital," but the next chapters will break down the approach, no matter who you are or what kind of organization you're leading.

The difference between digital transformation as it's often discussed and this Human-Centric Digital Transformation approach is the effort it takes to step out from behind the corporate abstraction to make sure human actors/players/constituents (employees, customers, stakeholders) have a say and have a future. It seeks to equip the digitized business with meaning as a tool for operational clarity as well as for better customer relationships.

The industry discourse about "digital transformation" has mostly dealt with replacing legacy systems, integrating data into decision-making, and reducing paper and other analog dependencies. But while we think about "transformation," we should also think about "integration." How every platform increasingly depends on others, and how the company leadership needs to consider multiple inputs from across channels, sources, and silos in order to make effective decisions.

And we need to think about the people who work, the people in the market, the people all along the way who play some part in the process.

We talk about "digital transformation," but most corporate environments are anything but transformative—unless you mean the power to transform a whole person into a compartmentalized fraction. We ourselves need to be integrated, ready to be transformed.

A completely machine-driven economy is an interesting thought experiment. What happens to human income? What happens to the value of human-to-human interaction? Does a cottage industry of human contact form outside of the machine-driven economy? But imminent market demands for efficiency must be met long before we reach that stage, and the role of humans must be part of the equation.

The following chapters will give you strategic tools to use with your own team to drive a meaningful and Human-Centric Digital Transformation with greater clarity and agility.

We will explore how to get the clear sense of focus and alignment you need, and in later chapters, we will explore how to put it into action.

Introducing the Human-Centric Digital Transformation Executive

Strategy Canvas

You have a lot to think about before you ever start thinking about rolling out new technology.

As I have advised clients about strategy and innovation over the years, they often have approached me with very tactical or one-dimensional questions, such as: How can we acquire more customers? How can we increase customer retention? And so on. In those situations, I want to guide the discussion to a more meaningful, purposeful, intentional, dimensional understanding of what we need the technology decisions to achieve, so I've used this canvas in executive workshops to meet that end.

According to the feedback I've received, the canvas provides great clarity. One workshop attendee, a CEO of a utility corporation, said that this canvas exercise helped him recognize an opportunity to investigate automating a particular component of their call center intake that would both increase efficiency and improve customer response time. The step would allow the company to shift some of the call center employees into roles overseeing the automation workflow and results, which would represent higher value to the company, bring higher pay to the employees, and potentially reduce some of the high-churn recruitment activity in the call center over the long term. The call center automation opportunity wasn't on his radar, but it became a top priority for the year. Perhaps sharing this methodology here can help more companies think through the impact of automation on staff and job roles in a sustainable and humane way, and can prompt ideas for re-purposing human talent into higher-value roles.

The clarifying work comes while you're trying to articulate the purpose statement. Once articulated, the purpose statement becomes a yardstick by which you can measure the relevance of your goals, priorities, resource allocation, and more.

Human-Centric Digital Transformation Strategy Canvas

CULTURE / BRAND / EXPERIENCE	Purpose Statement — *Why does your company exist, and what are you trying to do at scale?*				From Canvas to Roadmap
	Goals for this Year	Goals by Quarter	Purpose-Driven Priorities	Resources to Align/Re-Align	What levers can you pull to get more revenue, and what are the costs/tradeoffs?
	Values	Daily Actions	Big Question	Big Ideas	Data Model & Effectiveness
	Positioning relative to market		How can your brand bring your culture to life?		
	Whom do you serve?	How do they get value?	How can your experiences bring your brand to life?		Tech Deployment Possibilities

Human-Centric Digital Transformation Canvas

You can use this expression of purpose to help provide further clarity about the rest of your organization. Each of these sections will be examined further in this book, because only through alignment is a Tech Humanist approach possible.

In the second row, just below the purpose statement, are spaces to note annual and quarterly goals, because while some goals may be driven by circumstantial need, in general these should square up. If you review your goals in light of the purpose you've articulated and recognize some opportunity to shift emphasis, you can denote these in the spaces for purpose-driven priorities and resources to align or re-align.

The next row of spaces is for culture-related elements: such as values and daily actions. Gathering ideas together like this can illustrate something that may have long gone unsaid, such as a character trait that is prized within the company culture but which has never been formally stated as a company value. One team I worked with recognized integrity, for example, as a key characteristic they hired for and cultivated but had never stated was important. Also in this row are spaces for two consulting tools I use with clients: What is the big question you are trying to answer in your organization or with a given product? And what is the big idea that your organization puts forth into the world?

A well-defined organizational strategic purpose also helps shed light on aspects of the brand, but also a well-defined brand can help clarify purpose. It can be easier to recognize truth when it's in abstract or metaphorical terms. Here you can make note of your brand's positioning relative to the market, and how your brand can bring your culture to life.

In the bottom row are questions that relate to experience strategy: Whom do you serve? How do they get value? How can your experiences bring your brand to life?

Following these questions, in the righthand column, you can begin to envision a roadmap to accelerate this model. Having articulated all of this, do you see where you might have the opportunity to invest more to gain more? Do you see insights about what your data model should tell you about the effective running of your organization? Do you see how you might deploy technology to accelerate and amplify parts of the culture, brand, and experience?

Where to Begin with Digital Transformation?

It's common and far too easy to think about digital transformation in terms of wholesale automation or making every part of the business data-driven and algorithmically optimized. Most business publications and the mainstream media would have you believe digital transformation is about keeping up with the latest technology.

But that misses the point. Your business started for a reason, and it probably had something to do with making something. Something people would buy, use, need, consume, covet, and/or trust. Something they'd want in a singular way, that would resonate with some value you share with your audience. There are always more efficient ways to do business, but they don't always lead to making people come back to your business or recommend it to their friends. The key to human-centric digital transformation is knowing your business purpose so you can fulfill it more meaningfully at scale.

The key to Human-Centric Digital Transformation is knowing your business purpose so you can fulfill it more meaningfully at scale.

Digital transformation is largely about incorporating the right data points, and that data represents humans. So it's already about people.

In the sense that digital transformation is about deciding what technology is meaningful to your business strategy and to your customers' experience, it kind of is about keeping up.

But don't forget the mindset. It has to come from a place of mutual reward. Because human experience is changing all the time, your customers' expectations are also changing. You do have to keep up. The best way to know what tech to invest in is by thinking about your own organizational purpose and what emerging tech applications align with it and would amplify it to create a more meaningful experience for your customer.

The good news is: You only have to transform in your business what doesn't align.

Curiosity and an excitement about what's next have made my background wonderfully eclectic, but where it conceptually comes together is around experience strategy. I have built my expertise out of an education in languages and linguistics (i.e., how we communicate what is meaningful), early professional accomplishments in the Web and digital content (i.e., how we organize knowledge for meaningful use), and how data and empathy both inform strategy (i.e., what is meaningful about our business to those we serve).

With the emerging technology landscape changing every day, it's easy to be overwhelmed. Just trying to keep up with the latest developments in any one area—like artificial intelligence, blockchain, mixed reality, or the Internet of Things—can feel like a full-time job.

But it's not your full-time job. You have a business to run. And it's time to get serious about bringing it up to speed with current technologies.

But which ones?

Operationally, you may need to look at logistics systems, applicant tracking systems, financial modeling systems, or robotic process automation.

In your marketing, you may need to look at marketing automation, chatbots, and so on.

There are analytics packages for everything.

Two schools of thought emerge when it comes to any kind of project deploying new and experimental technology, and especially with automation and machine learning: Either start with something important, or start with something easy.

If you have a problem that matches both criteria, so much the better.

But there's something to be said for both, and it matters how your organization is wired. If you start with something "easy," and it turns out not to be easy or not to deliver big results (as it might not if it's relatively trivial in scope), will your organization tend to lose patience? If you're the CEO or business unit leader, be honest with yourself about this.

If that is likely to happen, then by all means, dig into a more weighty problem right away.

But do what you can to make sure it aligns with the organizational purpose. More on that next.

CHAPTER 20

Get Clear on Purpose

AS UNLIKELY AS IT SOUNDS, humans and machines share a common motivator. Humans thrive when they have a sense of meaning, of connection to something larger than themselves, of contributing to something significant. Machines thrive when they're given succinct instructions with a clear set of priorities. What both of these needs have in common is that they can best be accomplished by understanding why you're doing what you're doing. In other words, having a clear sense of purpose happens to align machine goals and human goals.

The word *purpose* is overused, and it carries an association with something spiritual or touchy-feely. Both of those connotations can turn leaders off. And it's easy to get purpose confused with mission statements or vision statements, but those tend not to be as clear.

Leading any kind of organization through any kind of digital transformation effort requires a clear sense of direction, but how can you be sure you're making the right calls and setting the right priorities?

The Tech Humanist approach relies on strategy alignment and integrated experience, and the key to both of these is the sense of purpose: the map that guides your actions. The following section

51

explores how purpose informs the Purpose Core, which includes culture and brand, and how these together inform decisions that shape your strategic decisions. This chapter will help you articulate the kind of clarifying strategic purpose and principles that help align priorities and resources so you can invest and adapt with confidence.

The Purpose Core: Purpose + Culture + Brand

How do we get to better business that drives technology that empowers humanity? How do we align the objectives of business and humans?

Well, to begin, we know we're tracking people's data, so maybe we can use people's digital information and behavioral data to sell more widgets and make more money. *Or* maybe we can invent cool things, solve people's problems, and create meaningful connections. *Or* maybe we can do both.

Let's do both. Right? Both/and. Integrated. That's the whole underpinning of the Tech Humanist idea.

So what does it take to do both? It takes being very clear about what it is we're trying to do.

In other words, we have to identify our purpose. Our organizational purpose.

I'm not talking about mission statements or vision statements, or any of that "leverage our synergies" quasi-language businesses are tempted to use. Often I find a vision statement has lost any real meaning after it took fifty revisions and three committees to approve it. (Iteration is the path to success for many things, but there's also truth to "death by committee." It isn't always fair to draw this as a dichotomy, though, since any kind of writing is usually truer in earlier drafts with fewer people and more palatable or polite in later revisions with more people.)

At its best, your strategic purpose statement is a 3–5 word distillation of what your business exists to do, and is trying to do *at scale*.

> Your strategic purpose statement is a 3–5 word distillation of:
> what it is your company exists to do,
> and is trying to do
> *at scale*.

Why is purpose the starting point? Because humans crave/seek/are compelled by/thrive on meaning. And meaning in business strategy takes the shape of purpose.

You start with purpose because it informs what you're trying to do at scale. The scale part matters: We talk about growing to scale, achieving scale, using scale to make sense of a business model that wouldn't make sense unless the company were operating at scale. "Scale" is sometimes a pretty abstract concept in business, more so than profit or growth. Profit and growth can both be measured with some certainty. Scale, on the other hand, is something you'll sort of know when you get there. It's also sometimes a relative concept; you function at scale relative to your earlier state or relative to other companies not as well-scaled as yours.

You start with a strategic purpose so you can develop a purposeful strategy. That may sound like a tautology, but I promise you that it is not.

STRATEGIC PURPOSE

leads to

PURPOSEFUL STRATEGY

I propose that what makes the difference in a Tech Humanist sense is whether you are achieving your purpose at scale.

Have you ever done a personal exercise where you ask yourself what your most important goals are? What you end up with may not be new or surprising, but it does feel true and clear. If you take that moment of renewed clarity to review your priorities and activities, you might find yourself decluttering and adding some more meaningful actions that will help you get where you want to be. At some level this exercise may seem reductive and repetitive, but it's about taking a step back to understand/remind ourselves what is meaningful to the audience. We can then use that clarity, that momentary awareness, to align and focus efforts and resources.

This effort is similar, but rather than focusing on a personal sense of purpose, it is about finding a common esprit de corps: a cohesive sense of what gets people excited to do the work the organization does (when it does what it's supposed to do).

A clear purpose is not usually something that originated in the boardroom — even if that's where you end up articulating it for the first time. Typically, it's something that resembles the origin story of the company, that goes beyond a simple assessment of profit, that drives at some deeper passion shared by the founders and the early employees — a need to change the world, answer a big question, provide a big service, offer a big idea, etc.

It really is as simple as: A clearer sense of strategic purpose leads to a more purposeful execution of strategy.

> A clearer sense of strategic purpose leads to a more purposeful execution of strategy.

This is how a strategic articulation of purpose leads to a purposeful articulation of strategy.

And if that strategy aligns with authentic cultural values, it can be rolled out and executed in dimensional ways that bring the brand to life in the market and make it meaningful and memorable and possibly beloved.

PURPOSEFUL STRATEGY

Purpose	Culture	Brand	Experience
3-5 word articulation that anyone and any project in organization can help fulfill	how is the purpose felt inside the company?	how does the purpose come to life outside the company?	what are the metaphors and touchpoints that can make this real?

But it's the purpose that comes first. The purpose helps shape culture and brand, and in turn they together shape the data model and the technology infrastructure that's needed to achieve the purpose at scale. Articulating the purpose first and making sure the culture is reflective of it will ensure that every part of the technology transformation is also reflective of the values and purpose intended. Now more than ever, with automation accelerating and amplifying every potential misstep and misalignment, the organization must strive to be aligned operationally in every possible way with that purpose and around that cultural imperative.

Because our goal is to use data and technology in such a way that it makes you more successful and creates more meaningful and dimensional experiences for the people who do business with you.

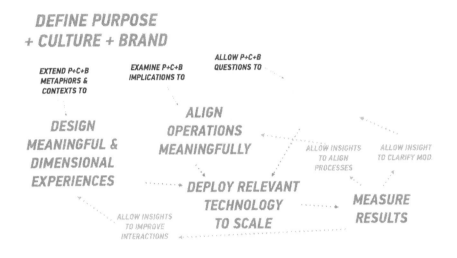

This is a premise I've held for years and years now—that a clear sense of purpose leads to better articulation of strategy, culture, and brand, more meaningful experiences, and ultimately more successful operations—and I've had the luxury of writing about it, speaking about it, consulting about it, and getting a chance to see it work and play out again and again.

Building A Meaningful Brand

Some brand experts talk about a brand as a promise. Some talk about the customer experience as the living embodiment of brand.

As much as anything else, a brand is a guardrail that, when

developed well and given proper placement, represents a metaphor of the company's purpose and values and guides a company's execution.

This is why brand matters in the Tech Humanist approach: because purpose is so central to integrating business objectives and human objectives, and brand is often a constantly visible reminder of that purpose. It helps keep efforts aligned.

Once you have articulated your values, how can brand bring your values and culture to life externally?

Then the next question is: How can operations amplify values, culture, and priorities internally?

How can the metaphors and contexts suggested by the purpose, culture, and brand be extended into experiences that resonate?

People can assume the company's origin story is something customers want to hear. Sometimes they do, when it's remarkable, when it establishes affinity with a value shared by brand and customers, when it demonstrates the founder's credibility in a significant way, or when it exemplifies the attributes of the brand promise or value proposition in a relevant way. An example might be Southwest Airlines: Herb Kelleher and the rebellious way he bucked convention and disrupted the airline industry.

But these origin stories are subject to evolving through their own mythology. The story Reed Hastings has told about Netflix has varied slightly in the retelling quite a few times. And all of the versions may well be true, representing different decisions along the founding journey or different obstacles they had to overcome. But if you hear Reed tell the story once and then hear a different version later, even if they're somehow both true, they'll both sound less credible.

Instead, focus on the problem the company is solving in the marketplace, the story of the brand, of the product, of the features. Nike has a fantastic origin story, but Just Do It as a brand promise and shared value is instantly more memorable and meaningful.

Disney Theme Parks and Magical Experiences

❈ ❈ ❈

One of my favorite examples of strategic purpose and alignment is the distillation to purpose of the Walt Disney Parks and Resorts. Their purpose is to "create magical experiences": a legacy that goes back to Walt Disney. (Often purpose is associated with a founder or other origin story.)

> "For years, Disney cast members talked of 'sprinkling pixie dust' to create magical experiences for their guests. But there is no line item for pixie dust on any Disney expense report. The pixie dust is the show that has been created—a show that runs at Walt Disney World from the moment guests arrive on the property until they leave for home."[15]

It starts with the clarity of mission, around which everything can align. Then notice that the emphasis is already on experiences. They want the experience to come first and to be memorable, share-worthy, etc., so that people will tell their friends and come back. (First-time Disney visitors have a 70 percent return rate.) A small increase in loyalty can mean huge returns on the bottom line.

And it has to do with processes, training, workflow, etc.—all kinds of internal operations.

As long as the management culture doesn't contradict it, clear purpose also dimensionalizes a culture of doing, of solving problems. You can imagine any employee at any level within the company being presented with a problem and feeling that they have the tools to solve it simply by asking, "How can I solve this in a way that creates the most magical experience?"

No one can anticipate all of the issues and real-world scenarios a product or service will encounter once customers start to use it, so one of the genius parts of alignment through purpose is that it motivates people to be part of living out the purpose and brand in responsive, dimensional ways.

Once those problems are solved in a way that feels true to purpose and aligns with an understanding of success (which includes customer satisfaction and loyalty, so it has to be win-win at some level), those solutions can become part of the playbook, codified into culture, part of the organizational knowledge, part of the corporate mythmaking.

You'd better believe Disney is collecting data to measure meaningful touchpoints. And of course, deploying relevant technology. After all, they were able to make a billion-dollar investment in the MagicBands that integrated—there's that word again!—visitor payment options, room access, preferences, and other data and information to make the park experience feel seamless and, indeed, magical.

The Southwest Airlines Standard for Strategy

For some time, Southwest Airlines has been every strategist's favorite example of a near-perfectly aligned company, and they are no less relevant in the Tech Humanist approach. Their purpose and brand is built around value and passing that savings along to customers, making customers part of the process and experience. Although they offer low-cost flights, the value proposition is not about being cheap; it's about involving customers in the decision to save money. It's a subtle distinction people sometimes don't get, but let's examine it.

First of all, their flight attendants are known for being fun (sometimes in a corny way, but still: not boring) and making the standard flight safety announcement with some funny personalized twists. They'll use a song or a rap, or something equally quirky. Southwest's stock ticker symbol is LUV, which is partly a nod to Dallas Love Field, their home base airfield, but also a reference to the friendly relationship they try to cultivate with passengers.

None of that has anything to do with offering a low-cost fare, but it does imply that everyone is in this together.

Southwest has operationalized their purpose, culture, and brand idea: They were built around a schedule of short-hop flights that made the schedule predictable, and they invested from the outset in a standardized fleet of airplanes to maximize the utilization of both flight crew and maintenance crew (meaning that everyone knows how to work on every plane).

And my personal favorite part of the story: the peanuts. In order to cut costs both to the airline and to passengers, they adopted a no-frills approach of not serving meals during flights. Instead, they offered peanuts. And peanuts are, of course, a metaphor for a small amount of money. As in: to work for peanuts, "It's peanuts to me," or, "That flight was so cheap, it was practically peanuts!"

As of August 2018, Southwest has stopped serving peanuts on their flights due to allergies—which is a wonderful act of inclusion and a nod to passenger safety. But I'll always have fond memories of the peanut days.

Their digital transformation efforts over recent years have been similarly focused on improving the passenger experience and streamlining their operations. Efforts to improve the simplicity of passenger flight changes and the reliability of baggage management[16] have been some of their tech improvement priorities.

Embedding Values into Culture

When you know the values you stand for as a company, you can look for ways to "encode" them into culture through policy and through management practices.

Perhaps the most viral example of this was the Netflix culture deck[17], created jointly by Patty McCord, the longtime Chief Talent Officer, and Reed Hastings, the founder and CEO. Their slide document was viewed more than five million times on the web[18], and it included deep references to the values they sought and cultivated. The company invests in hiring and retaining only "fully formed adults" who have good judgment, so they developed a lot of the policies to reflect a certain autonomy. The famous "no paid time off" policy comes from that line of thinking, where employees don't have to formally request PTO or adhere to a fixed amount of it. The implication was that professionals would communicate with their managers and teams about when they were taking time off, and that they would not take more time than necessary and manage their work with the excellence expected of them.

This may sound as though it doesn't relate to technology, but it sets the context of the work environment where values are being encoded into technology every day. Isn't it easy to imagine that a culture where employees are treated with dignity and respect is more likely to yield a product that treats its customers with dignity and respect?

Encoding these values is an intentional leadership choice.

In early 2018, Airbnb CEO Brian Chesky wrote an open letter to their user and host community about the vision the company had planned for an infinite time horizon, and serving all stakeholders.

> "A close advisor told me that now was the time to 'institutionalize your intentions so that even as you grow, you can minimize what conflicts with your vision.' It made me realize that we should write down what we want to institutionalize before it's too late. So I asked myself, if Joe, Nate and I were gone tomorrow, what would we want the world to know about Airbnb's intentions?"[19]

I loved that he said an advisor had told him to "institutionalize [his] intentions." Kudos to that advisor. Just after that, he also wrote: "Airbnb is still young, and the cement hasn't hardened." There's a lot of wisdom in realizing that culture and process tend to calcify, so it's easier to set those intentions earlier and develop them out into the work styles, relationships, brand, and experiences that represent your values than to reverse engineer an evolved system.

Strategic purpose yields powerful, purposeful strategy as it aligns the organization and leads to better results. It's the same idea.

Start with Empathy, Scale Through Meaning

We talk a lot about empathy in marketing, but in business terms, empathy alone doesn't offer a lot of insight. You need the effort of alignment to make it actionable and practical.

Analytics can expose patterns, but many of those patterns can be arbitrary. Beware arbitrary patterns. Just as absurdity sits in opposition to meaning, arbitrariness also sits opposite meaningfulness. We wouldn't want to codify things that happen to fit a pattern if they don't serve the alignment of business and human goals and/or the amplification of human values, or the enrichment of human experiences.

I'm a fan of nuance. I'm drawn to complexity and finding its meaningful patterns, as well as looking for broader patterns than what sound bites and simplistic models might suggest.

At the same time, what matters most to me is meaning, at every level from semantic to existential.

When I ran an optimization agency and we did A/B testing for clients on their websites, sometimes a test would have results that were completely different from what I or anyone predicted. Occasionally these results seemed immediately self-explanatory if, say, a channel was driving more of a particular behavior and we could easily imagine a narrative that might account for it. But occasionally the results were surprising *and* defied any kind of obvious narrative explanation.

I always saw the risk in both our tendency to develop a narrative to explain the results and in not questioning what the narrative might be.

If an insight that helps clarify the value of the product or offering to customers becomes apparent, then it's an opportunity to adopt that result in the context of that test.

But we must be careful about generalizing: Cautiously float that learning into the rest of the company as a possible higher-level insight.

Be wary of using algorithms to enforce arbitrary patterns, but also be wary of refusing to adopt a pattern that could be effective just because we can't explain it.

(See also Ethical considerations for discussion of the ethics of using AI-recognized patterns even when we can't explain them.)

Emphasis on Human Meaning in a Machine-Driven Future

So to make technology better for business and better for humans, we need to emphasize human meaning in a machine-driven future. The struggle is how to create a business rationale and strategy for a successful, scalable, future-ready digital transformation that doesn't lose sight of the human experience.

How do you ready your business for the future, guard against platform disruption, and embrace emerging technology when it's relevant?

It helps to remember that meaning isn't merely an altruistic principle when we think about its value to humans; it also benefits business. Meaning takes the shape of purpose, which allows for focus, prioritization, clarity of direction, etc., which ultimately facilitates growth, scale, profit.

There's something else too.

As we've already discussed, humans thrive on meaning, as well as a collective sense of contributing to something bigger than themselves. Whereas machines, given their rules-based processing, do best with clear and succinct instructions. And guess what leads to both of these? That's right: purpose. A clear sense of organizational strategic purpose achieves both.

If you can distill your objectives into language that paints an aspirational picture for humans and the basis for a set of no-nonsense guidelines for machines, you're well on your way.

In a study on workplace automation, McKinsey found that the amount of time that most workers spend on activities that require creativity and active empathy was low: Only 4 percent of activities required creativity, and only 29 percent required active empathy or sensing emotion.[20]

Their report drew similar conclusions to most like it, suggesting that the opportunity for higher-order work can expand as routine tasks become automated. As it does. But a Tech Humanist take is both/and: We should both want to free humans up for higher-order work *and* recognize that most existing work today could benefit from greater application of creativity and empathy. Because as more of that work becomes automated, the effort it will take not to merely automate mundanity but rather allow for even slightly more nuanced interactions between machine and human will be dramatic as those automated functions accrue around us.

Working from a clear sense of strategic purpose is truly the way forward for a Tech Humanist future.

CHAPTER 21

Integrate

EVERYTHING ABOUT THE TECH HUMANIST approach is integrative. By definition we are trying to create a world that integrates the best of technological possibility with the fullness of human potential. In exploring this approach, we are seeking positive business outcomes in a society that enriches human life.

So it stands to reason that one of the central tenets of tech humanism is integration. Building the potential for the best futures for the most people relies on integration of many kinds: integrated strategy, integrated interactions, integrated teams, and integrated mindsets. It means recognizing that more win-win scenarios exist than we typically admit to. It means examining every idea for what seems contradictory to it and considering whether an integrated approach might give the resulting experience more dimension.

Integration lends itself to dimensionality.

Both-And Thinking

❋ ❋ ❋

"The test of a first-rate intelligence is the ability to hold two opposed ideas in the mind at the same time, and still retain the ability to function. One should, for example, be able to see that things are hopeless and yet be determined to make them otherwise."
— *F. Scott Fitzgerald, "The Crack-Up," a three-part series in the February, March, and April 1936 issues of Esquire*[21]

The Tech Humanist approach is inherently an integrative approach. One way to think about it in practice is its quality of being "both/and" rather than "either/or." I'm a big believer in the power and wisdom of embracing a "both/and" mentality rather than an "either/or" mentality more often than not.

Because more often than not, while a simple articulation of a fundamental idea like "people are basically good" or "cash is king" works as a sort of koan, the most widely applicable insights tend to be multifaceted. It can be simultaneously true, for example, that focusing on one single metric can help align an organization's efforts *and* that relying on any one single metric is too shortsighted, narrow, and simplistic for a model that leads to scalable, sustainable success. Being able to hold seemingly conflicting ideas in your mind at the same time and knowing how and when to apply which interpretation and how they weave together to create an integrated truth is a critical skill for leadership, and a critical skill for life.

In my work with top companies on future-ready strategy, digital transformation, and the future of human experience, I'm increasingly seeing opportunities for integration. And integration is a key to unlocking the potential in the business models that adapt well to the future. Integration is a key theme in a lot of the world right now.

For example, looking through the lens of tech humanism encourages us to see humanity and technology as coexisting, as powerful forces that can work well together.

The opportunity with Human-Centric Digital Transformation is in empowering and enabling business to succeed with data and technology *while also* making it possible for humans to have a future full of more meaningful, fulfilling experiences.

I believe there's room for both data collection and privacy.

There's room for both competitive edge and collaboration.

There's room for trade secrets and transparency.

There's room for the complex work that needs to be done, and for clarity when it comes to human needs and outcomes.

Integrated Win

When something fits Tech Humanist principles and is a win for the business side, a win for the human side, and a win as a precedent for the responsible use of data and/or progress of technology, I call that an Integrated Win.

It's an expansive way of thinking, one that steers clear of deciding that there's only one right answer or one winner or one dominant part of society or one seat of power.

Business can be strong and powerful and a source of growth and employment and resources and conveniences for people...*and* it can engage in responsible, ethical, ecologically sustainable practices.

Online and Offline, Physical and Digital

A noticeable form of integration is that of the physical and digital worlds, of online and offline experiences, of what's "real" and what's virtual.

Of course I already wrote an entire book about it (*Pixels and Place*), but even in the short time since that book was published and as I write this one, so much has continued further down that road. More and more of our human experiences are crafted from data that we generate as we move through the world in both online and offline contexts.

Now more than ever, the distinction between online and offline is blurring. The data collected on one side informs the experiences created on the other. And as I've long said, just about everywhere interesting that the physical world and digital world connect, the connection layer is happening through our human experiences.

For more on how to design human experiences for these integrated online and offline contexts, see Integrated Human Experience Design.

Gig Economy, Changing Expectations of Work, Roles Not as

Distinct

The gig economy has also facilitated integration, where roles such as "consumer" and "employee" aren't as distinct as they used to be.

One way this is true is that the model is so distributed: Whole segments of people participate as workers in the gig economy, such as driving for ride-sharing services, while sometimes using the gig economy services themselves—perhaps even occasionally using the same ride-sharing service as a passenger.

But also because the employer-employee relationship isn't as fixed or permanent in the gig economy as it has traditionally been.

Some people take up gig economy jobs as side hustles, while others have replaced traditional jobs with a mix of gig work, such as taxi drivers who decide to drive for both Uber and Lyft because they can set their own hours. But that tradeoff also means they don't qualify for the benefits that have come with traditional jobs. Still others sign up to deliver for Postmates or tackle odd jobs through TaskRabbit or gather groceries for Instacart because they have struggled to find full-time work elsewhere.

Recent surveys show that 16.5 million people in the United States are in "contingent or alternative" work. Those may not all be "gig economy" jobs, but they're included in that number, and it's a significant enough total to merit our attention. The people working in these jobs often have few benefits or protections. And for sheer size of population, compare that number to the coal industry, which employs 80,000 Americans, or the steel industry, which employs 150,000.[22]

For context, we can look to the composition of individual annual tax filings. W2s are the forms typically used for traditional employees, although some temp and contract workers also file W2s, whereas 1099-MISCs would record payments to non-employees, such as those engaging in nontraditional, freelance, or gig economy work. Since 2000, the number of W2s fell by around 3.5 percent, while during the same period, the number of 1099-MISCs filed with United States tax returns shot up by about 22 percent. These are dramatic shifts in the nature and composition of work.

When we talk about the future of work, these are major considerations. Being aware and mindful of this change and the trend moving this direction is important as you consider the future of your own company's business model and strategy. If you run a company that creates a marketplace of gig labor and uses on-demand employees, consider the relationship you create with the humans who do the interim work as well as the humans who buy from you. A dignified, respectful relationship with all the human stakeholders in the economy goes a long way toward creating a sustainable, successful future for us all.

Global and Local, and "Glocal"

As the world moves toward a more global economy, we're seeing a renewed interest in and emphasis of local markets and ecosystems. I've seen it called "glocal," but I'll take neither credit nor blame for that term.

Examples are abundant in retail. For one, West Elm as a corporate brand has tried to connect its larger global brand and its local store markets. They showcase local artisans and makers at the store, amplifying them as they succeed at each level. At the same time, they form partnerships with other national brands that in some cases dimensionalize the value of both brands for their shoppers beyond what they could experience individually. For example, West Elm partnered with Casper mattresses, which had only been available for sale online, to feature the mattress in stores and allow shoppers who were already in a mindset to look for home furnishings to interact with the fast-selling mattress in a tangible way—while also, of course, bringing in shoppers who were curious about the brand into the store. Those customers would then be in a position to see and potentially purchase goods from the featured local artisans.

Consider the example set by the Nashville Fashion Alliance in reinforcing the local ecosystem for designers in ways that allow the designers to compete on a global level. While Nashville is perhaps best known for country music, the city and its surrounding Southeast region are home to the largest concentration of independent fashion brands outside of New York and Los Angeles.[23] Yet they were struggling to scale: NFA chief executive Van Tucker kept hearing from designers and others in the local fashion community that certain kinds of resource gaps, such as a shortage of skilled sewers, were creating growing pains and constraints. So the association worked with a local manufacturer, Omega Apparel, to create a sewing academy and partnered with Catholic Charities to allow participants, many of whom were area refugees, to go through the academy to learn new skills and gain certification. Omega even promised to hire a certain number of graduates from the program over the coming years. They needed the skilled work, too. Housing can be provided as well. The program is so brilliantly devised, it truly benefits everyone involved and is a boon to the local economy. Everyone prospers more than if they were trying to solve their individual problems on their own.[24]

The Open Data movement connects to this idea of integrated global/local value in several ways. Some data sets come from government or other public sources that aggregate local census information, environmental and geological surveys, and so on, as well as from other private business sources. Yet the data can be used within a global initiative to represent insights for that locality or directionally as part of broader trends. It may be cross-referenced with other big data sets that can be sliced and diced to find local insights. The resulting output can yield big insights for business, and in many cases useful protections, opportunities, and tools for humans.

Smart cities initiatives are often precisely this mix of what has been learned and observed in other regions adapted for what works in a particular locale. Data sets that shed light on urban migration, the effects of climate change, traffic patterns, and public health are just some of the means by which a big-picture and hyperlocal view can be merged to benefit the people living in the place.

How could that trend and transformation play out within your industry? Within your organization? For the people who do business with you and rely on your products and services?

Tech + Human, or Business Goals + Human Interests = Better Experiences, Better Insights

All of this both/and thinking leads us back to why we are here: the blending of tech and human, of business goals and human interests, the integrative approach resulting in better experiences and better insights.

We now face the challenge of pulling back from our organizations, from our immediate problems and concerns, and looking at the ecosystem we're part of, or that we *could* be part of.

The big wins are in supply chain thinking, but also in disrupting the traditional view of supply and demand as a zero-sum landscape that limits the options for who can win. In fact we can't think merely in terms of winners and losers.

It's like the principles in negotiation of distributive versus integrative bargaining. In distributive approach, each person is arguing for their own best interest and outcomes. In an integrative approach, each party looks for a solution that benefits everyone.

Business has been applying business goals and metrics to human well-being for a long time. Great efforts are already being made to monetize healthcare, education, and so on.

But less explored, and potentially even more powerful, is the integrative opportunity to consider human well-being as it relates to business goals—and the long-term advantages and sustainability of doing so.

Greater Interactivity, Greater Engagement, Greater Insights

Part of what the Tech Humanist approach challenges us to do is look beyond the obvious for big opportunities to achieve Integrated Wins. Creating an experience that stands out as memorable requires asking what's expected within the context, and not only meeting it but exceeding it.

The fashion company Badgley Mischka demonstrated this when they promoted an interactive app at New York Fashion Week for audience members both at the event and watching remotely to engage with the looks as they came down the runway.

> Show-goers had the ability to "like" or "love" looks on the app as they came down the runway. In less than 10 minutes, the designer obtained quality feedback that would normally take six months to receive.

> Additionally, the results were surprising to Badgley Mischka—a black dress they weren't expecting to top the charts ended up being the second most popular item.

> Reimagining consumer engagement has launched Badgley Mischka one step ahead of the competition. These insights can now allow them to determine which styles to bring to market first and gauge how much to produce based on the popularity of each look. This helps prevent the production of low-popularity items, matching supply with demand to save on costs and reduce waste.

> — Digitalist Mag[25]

A win on insights for the company, and a win for audience members who perhaps wanted to participate in the process and keep track of the looks they were interested in. Introducing interactivity through apps, texting, kiosks, or other interactions is a huge opportunity.

Operational Clarity & Alignment

If your organizational purpose is, say, "to empower small business with efficiency," but your employees regularly have hour-long meetings that everyone dreads, there's a disconnect going on — and it will most likely amplify itself in the machine-driven experiences you create for customers. It will creep in. And the Tech Humanist mission will be impossible to achieve.

While brand and customer experience are the purpose brought to life *outside* the company, culture and operations should be the purpose brought to life *within* the company. So once you have articulated your organizational strategic purpose, you can use it to review and revisit all kinds of operational implementations of it. You can ensure that processes align with purpose, that workflow makes sense, that training adheres to the principles set forth by purpose, that hierarchy reflects the values implicit in that purpose, and yes, even that meeting length and frequency reflect purpose.

It's helpful to speak out loud what is probably known at a subconscious level about what aligns everyone's motives (including customers and employees).

Do your best to model this in data and capture some directional indicator of this alignment. Figure out how to model meaningfulness in data and operations. For example, if you can articulate purpose like Disney's, how do you assess on a regular basis that your organization is "creating magical experiences"?

You can leave it up to each division and department to define their own metrics and benchmarks, provided this approach works within your organization. That has the added benefit of pooling insights, including diverse perspectives, and getting everyone's buy-in to the work to be done. I go further into this when I discuss my experience at Netflix in Defining a Meaningful Data Model.

Here the big opportunity is not just for cost reduction, but for true alignment and clarity. Not just to optimize for efficiency and effectiveness but for amplification of values, purpose, and meaningful experiences. If that sounds too abstract, it's only because it needs to be grounded in operations. The opportunities are immense when you tie the higher-level strategic purpose into everything about your organization and its day-to-day work habits, rhythm, and operational flow, from internal project collaboration to supply chain visibility to workflow management and beyond.

Operations planning and supply chain management allow a tremendous amount of ethical power to amplify values.

On the human side of the equation, we don't always think about the world on the other side of our touch screens. But we can change the world around us with the smallest of interactions. It's so simple to place an order for a product (well, with some online retailers it's simple —perhaps not as simple with others), but it's easy to forget about or overlook the connected series of automated processes we set in motion, sometimes spanning the whole world, with a tiny tap of our fingertips.

As humans who consume in a globally connected economy, we all have an ethical obligation to be more aware of the human impacts of what we buy and what we set in motion. When our purchases can enable dehumanizing work conditions somewhere in the world—such as child labor or human trafficking—we need to demand transparency.

But for those of us leading companies that provide products and services, and for those selecting partners, vendors, and suppliers of all kinds for those companies, we have an ethical obligation to the humans who buy from us as well as to the humans impacted by the sequence of events enabled by those purchases. You may not directly control the factories where sweatshop conditions or child labor are being enforced, but you have a choice about whether to do business with them and empower them economically.

You can use strategic purpose to help you focus on the right annual and quarterly goals, to align values, goals, and priorities, and to determine where tech investments should be made.

It may mean doing at least a minimum of reorganization and reallocation of resources, human and otherwise. You may need to re-train people for different skill sets. You may need to divest equipment and buy new stuff.

How can your processes, policies, workflow, reporting structure, meeting schedule,

EVERYTHING

align with your stated purpose, culture, and brand?

Expanded Workforces: Remote, Virtual, Augmented

Today's business managers and leaders need to be ready to run projects and teams comprised of employees and non-employees, located locally and remotely, with both human and machine contributors. How on earth can a workplace adapt and prepare?

Other books and resources can dig into this in a more dedicated way, but it's important to address this within the context of how tech enables business and how that enablement can empower humanity. What will it mean, good or bad, to people who are working for this company as it makes this transition? What will the resulting experience look and feel like?

Leaders should not let the human experience — either inside or outside the company — suffer for lack of centralized guidance.

Certainly a company's location matters less and less from a logistics perspective, but on a cultural level, the choice of place is nuanced and dimensional. Going back to the importance of place, the best role a company's location can play is as a meaningful mechanism for extending the culture, values, and even the mythology of that location. So companies that have some significance to, say, music in Nashville (where I lived for twelve years before moving to New York) are bound to feel like natural parts of the landscape, and even though the race for tech talent is competitive there, much of the pool of talent in Nashville lives there because they're passionate about music. So if you're hiring a software developer for a music tech company and she just happens to love playing guitar, you've got a much more likely cultural fit than if your company were hiring somewhere else.

The Tech of Hiring Humans

❋ ❋ ❋

Even in a time when people are justifiably anxious about losing jobs to automation, hiring humans is still a function that takes an average of twenty-three days per new hire[26]. The effort to source, screen, interview, and decide on hiring people is labor-intensive enough that it is understandably a focus of automation and digital transformation efforts.

Technology solutions are emerging across the entire lifecycle of recruiting, hiring, human resources management, and retention.

Data can transform your hiring in meaningful ways if you are intentional with it. It can help your company dimensionalize culture, conduct resume matching by identifying what characteristics are meaningful to the company, prioritize inclusivity, and include diverse perspectives and thinking.

Moreover, the changes technology brings about are existential opportunities to rethink parts of the hiring and staffing process.

Knowing that certain kinds of artificial intelligence or robotic automation processes may turn out to be more effective and/or reliable and shake up the way we think about hiring for those roles, it could be useful in those disciplines to **hire for overall value, not just for skills**. In other words, perhaps good judgment and the ability to detect patterns and make meaningful additions will be more valuable in the long term than the specific skills that are likely to become augmented by machines.

Similarly, it may make sense to **hire beyond today's job functions**. There are bound to be jobs in the near future that don't exist or exist very rarely today as a result of digital transformation, automation, and artificial intelligence: roles such as nuance engineers, collections curators, or algorithm tuning. Such roles will be needed to keep the human in the machine-driven experiences.

Companies will probably also want to **hire for adaptability**. How quickly can this person learn? How easily can they adapt to the evolving needs of the company?

Another relatively recent change to recruiting and staffing is the ease with which distributed teams can collaborate and be managed remotely. The tools to assist with this setup continue to evolve, but it means that you can address talent shortages in technology roles creatively.

And as automation displaces and replaces human jobs, a tremendous opportunity to repurpose human skills and qualities to higher value roles develops, where characteristics like nuance, judgment calls, and contextual decision-making are important to the company's success and not easily replicated through automated systems or machine learning.

In short, do what it takes to make sure you're not overlooking the nuance in recruiting and hiring.

Nuances are not AI's strong suit. (Yet.) But humans do nuance well. We are generally pretty good at it. Not everyone picks up on all the nuances all the time, of course. But typically, we can detect layers upon layers of it.

After all, nuance is meaning—and we're wired for meaning. The challenge is to make sure we're encoding all the tools we can with the meaning we can detect.

For example, Mya, the recruiting app—and there are many others like this—promises to handle high-volume filtering at scale with some level of interpretation.

It's your call whether you set them up to answer candidate questions about what the coffee situation in your break room is like.

So you can parse résumés with natural language processing and information extraction, and deploy AI agents to screen candidates. As long as the objectives of the tool are aligned with the purpose and objectives of the company as a whole.

And of course you can do all kinds of other human resources–related functions with data and technology beyond screening résumés, such as facilitate performance reviews, conduct surveys, offer training, field complaints, and so on.

Well-designed tools can even push us past our biases. That includes unconscious biases, even those that seem initially positive, such as the affinity bias, where people unconsciously prefer people who seem to be like them in some way that doesn't necessarily have to do with job performance or true company values. Affinity bias is pervasive and manifests itself frequently in hiring decisions, when managers seek "culture fit" that's more about finding out, say, that they like the same beer. Resultant hiring mistakes cost the company diverse perspectives. Achieving a true culture fit means doing deep examinations of what culture really means for the company, and what value people add to the team when they are like-minded but bring different backgrounds or personality traits. Diversity of backgrounds on a team not only feels good and is the right direction to pursue, but it leads to significant improvements to the bottom line. Diverse firms have been shown to be more innovative, with more diverse companies 45 percent more likely to enjoy growth in market share and 70 percent more likely to break into new markets[27]. A 2009 study also showed that companies with more racial diversity had fifteen times more sales revenue than those with low racial diversity[28].

It stands to reason that the whole field of hiring and managing humans is in transformation due to technology. Now it's up to us as Tech Humanists to make sure we deploy the right technology to make the human work experiences and contributions as meaningful as possible.

Supply Chain, IoT Sensors, Automation, Other Tech Impacts on

Operations

Automation technology, IoT sensors, blockchain, and other emerging technologies are making huge impacts on supply chain tracking, logistics, and so on within operations management.

One of my favorite examples of this was a project undertaken by Siemens, who worked with a European train operator to model its train maintenance needs predictively. Using an array of sensors to gather data such as pressure and temperature from three hundred train components, they tracked their need for maintenance and managed the data in the Teradata platform. This "Internet of Trains" data project eventually led to recognition of a pattern that led to predictive insights, which could mean anticipating breakdowns before they happened. The impact of being able to assess wear in advance and maximize the time the trains are in service and minimize the cost, risk, and other effects of part breakdown is enormous.[29]

Think as well of the impact of 3D printing on supply chain and enterprise resource planning. Heck, if an astronaut on the International Space Station could 3D print a custom wrench to conduct repairs, there can't be many limitations on what can happen within your company.

Blockchain and IoT sensors offer greater transparency in the supply chain. They let people know your commitment to availability, deliverability, and sourcing, which means you can cascade your values and culture through your supply chain.

The fashion brand Rebecca Minkoff evaluates the vendors in their supply chain and holds them accountable to ensure their labor standards are sufficiently high and to keep from inadvertently supporting human trafficking and slavery. Their website includes a supply chain disclosure to assures customers of these high standards[30].

All kinds of opportunities exist in procurement, too, between blockchain-powered solutions, the Internet of Things, Robotic Process Automation (RPA), and AI. Companies can streamline and synchronize information throughout the supply chain for greater visibility, accountability, and control. This means massive changes in retail and beyond, for delivery, distribution, automation and warehouses, and so on.

You can use logistics to track an item's history, which has interesting applications in the grocery and restaurant businesses, where food often travels long distances to end up on your plate. A QR code can track their travels, which can lead to reduced inefficiencies and waste.

Consider the technological means of improving resource distribution. A potentially Tech Humanist example of this is Karma, a Stockholm-based start-up that, through an app-based marketplace, helps distribute unsold food from restaurants and grocery stores directly to consumers.[31] It launched in 2015 and lists over 1,500 food merchants, including bakeries, hotels, and cafés. The surplus food listed through the directory is sold to 350,000 users.

Other start-ups with promising approaches to improving the food-related supply chain through technology are Shelf Engine, which uses machine learning to help groceries managing their ordering to reduce the food waste in their own stores[32], and Full Harvest, which offers a B2B solution for reducing food waste[33].

The importance of all of this to the Tech Humanist picture is that people's expectations are changing, and with accelerating expectations comes additional need for convenience and time saving (or at least the perceived need).

How can you use this capability to help better align the business? How can you use it to align business needs and customer needs? How can you use it to make people's lives better?

CHAPTER 22

Make Experience Meaningful

YOUR BUSINESS HAS TO BE able to make decisions about focusing its resources, navigating the complexities of competitive digital business models and the opportunities and mandate to innovate and scale accordingly, staying out of the muddy waters of customer complaints on social media, and keeping a talented workforce engaged and motivated. How on earth do you do all of that?

You focus relentlessly on improving the human experience.

But whose job is it to think deeply about this for the organization? Who is accountable for it? The CEO? The CMO? Or is it a new role that we could call the "Chief Tech Humanist Officer"? "Chief Meaning Officer"? Or "Chief Purpose Officer"?

I'm a sucker for a fun title, but I don't think any of that is necessary. It's a set of responsibilities that belong everywhere, but arguably don't fall to any one part of the organization.

We talk a lot about user experience and customer experience, but those are siloed. The UX/CX conversation doesn't address three nuanced, multidimensional truths of the matter: 1) There are many contextual considerations for every person who engages with your company; 2) There are many humans involved in the process of helping your company succeed who are not customers, and their experience matters too; and 3) No matter what happens with machines and robots in the future, as long as there are humans and business, there will always be human stakeholders in business. So it behooves us to think about the universals of human nature as they relate to our business ambitions, and to make our businesses reflect the broadest ambitions of humanity.

Increasingly, businesses are tracking people's data well outside of any kind of consideration that looks like a purchase intent path. Which means businesses are involving themselves in people's lives outside of the brand-customer relationship. So companies need data practices that exercise the utmost care and caution with personal data, and a human experience mindset that considers the whole of a person who sometimes behaves as a customer and otherwise may not. There is a larger, longer-term, more holistic relationship to be developed, if a brand is willing to put in the work to model it and be conscientious about it.

Human experiences go well beyond the roles of user, customer, patient, and student. Stepping back from those roles allows us to look at the larger landscape of our humanity, our responsibilities, the additional roles we play, and the baggage we carry into our interactions. The most meaningful strategy thinks beyond the customer context to a holistic human experience that blends online and offline interactions, that acknowledges context broader than purchase intent, and builds lifetime value through relevant and respectful use of data.

Customer experiences specifically must rise above the mundane to be memorable, and to do so they must integrate physical and digital. Every day our physical surroundings and our digital interactions converge more and more through data analytics, connected devices and the Internet of Things, wearable technology, geo-tagged and geo-targeted social media, surveillance, sensors and beacons, and so on. In very real ways, our human experiences create a targeted feedback loop, defining our opportunities, our relationships, our knowledge, and, ultimately, our selves.

We increasingly experience integration and automation in the future of human experiences. We are the connective tissue that creates the data layer connecting physical and digital.

Our digital selves are our aspirational selves, in the sense that the interactions and transactions we engage in are part of the idea of who we are and most want to be, and social platforms and other companies track and use this data.

(And be clear, transparent, and forthright in your interactions with humans about their data: Google still recording many people's locations even after they turn off location tracking.)

This could mean giving people access to their own data. A number of start-up companies have launched, such as digi.me and Personal, which merged in 2017[34], to offer people the opportunity to create secure collections of their personal information in one place and selectively share it with companies.

Many platforms, including Facebook, offer data downloads for users of the service, which serves as both a backup of your online profile and an archive package you can take with you if you leave. Google also packs up the data you have across its service.

Bear in mind, the bare minimum is making the data available; to be a useful service, that data must be portable to some other application or platform, so it should ideally be available in a format that is an existing standard for use or convertible into that standard.

Now that machines are encroaching on everything everywhere, we need to know that when we interact with machines, we will be given respect or the semblance of respect.

Clearly, the implications of making experience meaningful go well beyond marketing and move into all aspects of how the business aligns and operates for the best chance of a meaningful interaction with the marketplace, a meaningful workplace, and a meaningful contribution to culture.

If you as a business can create interactions with me as a customer that make me feel you understand me and are trying to help solve my problems even as you benefit from my purchases, you will have created a potentially very powerful link between us.

It starts from understanding what drives the human behavior in the first place, or what holds it back.

Amazon recognized the friction customers experienced when considering shipping costs in making an online purchase. So they introduced Prime in 2005, which changed the economics of the business—and, it's not hyperbole to say, the American economy. While over half of American households hold Prime memberships, the number skews even higher for high-income Americans: 70 percent of American individuals with incomes of $150,000 have them.[35] Amazon now represents 49.1 percent of all US online retail spend, according to a July 2018 study[36]. Customers spend more money with Amazon than with all of its online competitors combined. (Walmart, which is the largest retailer due to its physical presence, only clocks in at 3.7 percent of spend online in the same study, although its 2016 acquisition of Jet.com did increase its internet market share and may yet improve its digital readiness.)

You wouldn't find Netflix where they are today if they didn't have their subscribers at the center of their thinking.

The phenomenon now known as "binge-watching" didn't really exist until the '90s, and it may have started with DVD box sets of TV shows—but it didn't change culture until Netflix began streaming in 2006/7/8 and the idea of "staying home to watch Netflix" actually became an idea.

Alibaba saw an opportunity and introduced Singles' Day in China, . It became the world's biggest shopping day, with online and offline sales reaching over $25.4 billion on November 11, 2017. They tapped into a dimension of human experience—buy yourself something—and created a massive business opportunity.

Any company can learn from this, find a dimension of human experience to relevantly amplify, and change culture. I encourage companies to do it from a place of aligned business and human objectives.

To find our way into this integrated future, we must explore the relationship between meaning, intention, data tracking, and human experience, and see if we can come back with practical insights on how businesses can harness data and technology to create innovative experiences that form the basis of more meaningful and profitable relationships with customers.

There are clues to meaning in what people value, and in what we know about their interest in what we offer. An integrated approach seeks to find further alignment. The goal of any digital transformation program should be to empower learning across the organization so it can further align with human experience.

Why Human Experience Matters

Due to our self-conscious self-awareness, we humans tend to see ourselves in the center of it all, but objectively we enjoy no special place in the lineup of life. That very same consciousness of our own existence grants us the potential for a special understanding of life, though, and arguably the ethical requirement to use it.

We talk about "what separates us from the animals," and we'll eventually have to think about "what separates us from the machines."

I think nonhuman animals deserve good experiences, too.

Soon enough we're going to have to think about robot experience.

Although I try to treat them nicely, I don't ascribe sentience to things like my coffee mug or my clothes. I want them to be in good shape and to last.

If the computer I use for the majority of my daily tasks were sentient, or very nearly so to the point where I couldn't be sure if it wasn't, I would want to treat it well, too, not only so it would last and be in good shape, but so that it might have a good experience.

When do we start to care about that?

In the meantime, we have to be concerned with actual human beings' experiences. And I don't just mean the users of the software we design and sell, or the customers of our products. I mean all the humans, everyone in the world, to the extent that we're able to have any influence on all humans' lives.

We have to consider diverse human experiences—which in practice within most of technology development we've taken to mean gender and racial inclusivity, and even then we're still not very good at it. But those diverse experiences include neurodiversity and cognitive differences. People living in famine and refugee conditions, and really all kinds of conditions imaginable. If we care about a "humanist" outcome, we need to cultivate an interest in the outcomes for all humans that result from the development, manufacture, and consumption of any experience. People working in sweatshops are every bit as human as you.

In other words, we have to be careful how we think about what human is, or else a "subhuman" area emerges.

Meaning should not be a privileged outcome. It's a fundamental aspect of humanity; therefore it should be a fundamental goal for human experience.

What I mean by meaningful experiences is those that have depth and memorability, that are significant because of how they transcend their context or complement their context.

> Meaningful experiences are those that have depth and memorability, that are significant because of how they transcend their context or complement their context.

All kinds of meaningful experiences: memorable, dimensional, transcendent, spiritual, existential, and so on.

What we experience changes us.

And everything is changing. Always.

If you're going to change it anyway, make it better.

We have a chance to put the right kind of experiences in place before they become crystallized through automation and learned process and subsequently hardened into routine and culture.

Decrease Customer Acquisition Costs

Although I prefer to default to a "human experience" orientation rather than "customer experience" or "user experience" when advising companies about strategy, it doesn't mean that I don't believe in the value of customer experience investments and programs. After all, customer experience *is* human experience when the human context is **deciding to buy**.

In the framework of customer experience, the best measurable evidence of true success is loyalty in the form of repeat business or advocacy in referrals or recommendations, but decreasing friction overall is tantamount to increasing customer loyalty. Making it simpler for someone to get from first contact with the brand to the point of purchase is generally the clearest way to both greater profits and a more satisfying interaction for the person doing the buying. There are direct returns to be gained by improving the customer experience in this way.

There's an average way to get there, and a Tech Humanist way.

The shortsighted way companies sometimes try to achieve success in this area is by pushy tactics like deceptive user interfaces, annoying follow-up email sequences, retargeting campaigns, and so on.

The Tech Humanist way to achieve these aligned improvements is about clearing obstacles for the customer, making the value proposition clear, and continually seeking relevant opportunities to add more value. The more holistically a company looks at their customer experience, the more improvements they stand to make.

We've been talking for years about omnichannel and digital transformation, but we haven't seen many brands successfully making sense of all this when it comes to making things easier for the people who want to buy from them. My biggest interest is in how much of an opportunity exists in integrating physical and digital experiences. I do see quite a few companies looking for ways to anticipate points of friction and using tools to ease them, whether it's online or offline or wherever. The solutions are high-tech or low-tech—but they're using the resources at their disposal to align the brand's objectives and the customer's objectives.

For example, for companies that are doing a lot of top-of-funnel interest-building work online but often need customers to close in person, such as car brands, they may be looking for ways to make their listings more reliable and even use better photography or other content to reduce customer uncertainty about carrying the process a step further.

Sometimes the backend work that supports better content or more robust and consistent metadata is just as important to the customer experience as something more overtly in the customer's purchase path. In an e-commerce context, the ability for a person to whittle search results down to what they're looking for can mean the difference between success and abandonment.

For example, I wear a size 11 shoe. Many women's brands only run up to 10, so shoes in my size are not always readily available. I often browse online shoe stores and find that the lack of ability to filter the product catalog by whether the style is available in my size is a make-or-break feature. But unless the retailer offers a size filter, I don't know whether any individual style happens to be available in my size until I've clicked into a few individual product listings and given up in frustration. Those same shoe retailers may even carry a few styles in my size, but it doesn't do anyone any good after I've gotten frustrated and left the site because they didn't make it easy for me to find some shoes.

Another delightful example of metadata enriching the shopping experience is the clothing rental business Rent the Runway. The fact that most women's clothing lacks pockets is a subject often lamented, and as a result, many women cherish clothing with pockets. (Real pockets, not tiny fake pockets.) So I was pleased recently to see that Rent the Runway had a metadata option in their faceted search for dresses for a "pockets" feature. I tweeted about it and learned in response that two software engineers at the company, Hindi Kornbluth and Madeline Rae Horowitz, built the feature as a "hack week" project because it was something they wanted themselves[37]. I find their dedication to the feature makes it even more charming, but one way or the other, there must be hundreds of little flourishes brands could make through data, through simple tools, or through whatever ability they have that can make the company goals and the customer needs harmonious.

Reducing customer friction is just another way to say aligning the company's objectives and the customer needs—and doing so in practice, iteratively, with discipline and dedication. That will certainly build brand loyalty, but there's an even more fundamental reason to do it: It requires the company to think deeply about alignment and how the company's goals can be carried out dimensionally through the products and services they offer. The brand can't stop at the obvious; the more they think through the layers and layers of opportunity to surface nuances of value between the company and customer, the more fully the company will be delivering on its own purpose as well as providing more meaningful experiences for customers.

Differentiated Experience Is Worth Investing In

Most experiences are forgettable; and from your perspective as a business leader, if they are more expensive, you're overpaying for attention. Meaningfulness may be hard to measure, but memorability is a proxy for meaningfulness.

Domino's Pizza created the experience of everywhere ordering by facilitating mobile ordering through smartphones, smart watches, and smart TVs.

CVS integrated the Curbside app for ordering products ahead and picking them up.

In the competitive landscape of consumer airlines, JetBlue Airways has differentiated by investing heavily in its operations and infrastructure to improve passengers' experience; deploying high-speed WiFi internet and streaming and making it free on all domestic United States flights[38]; offering mobile payment options for snacks and other premium in-flight selections[39]; and a variety of other features and tools.

It pays to have your experience stand apart from others in a meaningful way, but the only way to meaningful differentiation is through an understanding of purpose and alignment.

You can create the future you want by investing in what amplifies the alignment of your purpose and your customers' objectives. It helps to understand the dimensions on which that alignment happens. That's what we'll look at next.

Dimensionalize

It's easy to understand the relationship between a business and a customer in one dimension: transactions.

Beyond that is a dimension of "almost": Did the person *almost* become a customer? Did the business *almost* make the sale? Did the product *almost* satisfy the person's need? Did the message and offering *almost* convince them?

How many times are these "almosts" happening?

What is the dimension on which they are happening? The plane on which the human and the business approach each other but the alignment is ever so slightly off. Typically, the only way those missed connections are measured is within the dimension of transactions, when they're known, as lost opportunities that are missed revenue for the business.

But for every business, multiple levels exist on which it functions. Think of Netflix and its appeal as a lazy person's dream for binge-watching. Netflix is also a more intimate and controllable way of viewing your favorite movies and shows (who doesn't appreciate the ability to pause a movie when they go to the bathroom?), and a discovery tool for new movies.

And that's just the primary offering and the primary audience. That's not even getting into the relationships with studios and distributors.

What matters, then, is context. When you design for human experience with dimensionality, you can simultaneously enrich that experience while simplifying it, *and* ensure a better chance at a successful business outcome.

A more dimensional approach to experience design might also include an awareness that decisions and actions are often happening for people beyond *this* transaction in *this* instant, somewhere else off the platform, and integrating that context as much as possible by bringing it to the platform to reduce complexity for people. That might look like weather forecasts in travel booking apps, measurement tools in furniture catalogs, driving directions to an offline pickup location for an online purchase, and countless other variations.

When designers at Facebook began recognizing a pattern of people posting to ask for recommendations in a place, they tested features that would add more structure to the responses and make them more useful. For example, someone might post the ever-popular, "In New York for the day. Where's the best place to get a traditional slice?" (In my experience, that question tends to elicit lengthy and heated debate.) The Facebook team eventually developed tools using Conversational

AI and Natural Language Understanding (see also the section that further explains Machine Learning, Deep Learning, Conversational AI, Natural Language Processing) to parse the intent from the words a person might use in their post, allowing the platform to recognize a request and format it into a map displaying those recommendations. That seemingly simple process organizes what could easily be a frustrating or overwhelming thread of pizza joints into a map, so the person asking can perhaps choose an option that's not too far out of their way. (No guarantees on the quality of the slice, though.)

The more thoughtfully you dimensionalize people's experience, the easier you make it for them to follow the transaction path that leads to success for you. And life becomes just a little bit easier for everyone.

Augmented Humans, Augmented Life

A massive opportunity for technology in the context of human experience is to augment or enhance our human capacities and experiences to overcome limitations, to shape them in ways that are more to our tastes or more meaningful in some way.

Wikipedia, for example, is arguably already knowledge enhancement—as has been all of the internet and the World Wide Web, in some sense, for decades. The fact that our computer screens have been able to connect to repositories of human knowledge is already an awe-inspiring form of human augmentation.

Language barriers have fallen significantly, too: Machine translation, while sometimes still hilariously crude, is widely integrated into browsers for at least serviceable translations of content as we encounter it, and standalone apps like Google Translate are a godsend to travelers in countries where they don't speak the language or just feel they could use backup for reassurance. (Although I speak *some* Spanish, for example, the dialect I've acquired in the US is different enough from what's spoken in Barcelona that while visiting there I often felt far more comfortable trusting the app to speak for me, even realizing its substitutions might be awkward or slightly off, rather than relying on my vocabulary and regional pronunciation alone.) These capabilities enhance us, add to the fullness of our potential as individuals and as a society, make us more adaptable in the world, and can even reduce our anxiety.

And that's just the beginning of what is possible. Additional devices and tools will augment our senses in ways that will overcome human limitations and impose our own preferences on the way we interact with the world. That will shape our experiences. (You can read more about this ideas in Consider Both Nature and Shape of Experiences.)

How can tools of augmentation benefit humanity, or at least everyday human life? Doesn't it make sense that if you're already having a meaningful experience, that a tool that can help you understand it, identify it, and potentially reproduce it would be valuable?

It's one thing to take a stroll through a park, but what if you get curious about a beautiful tree you encounter and want to know what kind of tree it is? Isn't it nice that there are apps that can help you do that[40]? While you probably know there are apps that can help you identify songs, did you know there are apps that can help you identify birdsong[41]? Tools that can deepen human experiences and quality of life in small but meaningful ways have only just begun.

Speaking of apps that identify songs, while Shazam has been around as a song recognition tool since 1999, the features beyond real-time song recognition may not be as familiar to most people. The company expanded their capabilities to visual recognition in 2015, meaning that a user of the app could scan a book, say, or a product package and be directed to additional information and special offers. In 2017 they followed up with AR integration. Their brand partners could now use "Shazam Codes" on printed marketing materials and offer the app's user an in-the-moment offer and contextual experience, such as scanning a liquor bottle and seeing recipes for cocktails.

Moreover, a huge opportunity for emerging technology to augment human life is in public safety. If nanotechnology-based biosensors can detect a biohazard[42], if AI can diagnose cancer growth with imaging data that is invisible to the human eye[43], or if AI can identify the existence of a crack in a nuclear reactor[44], and thus benefit human life, isn't using technology this way an ethical imperative?

Even solving problems on a much smaller scale: Amazon acquired an AR start-up called Partpic and integrated it into their shopping app in the camera function, so now, with the Part Finder feature, you can identify a screw from your washing machine and easily find a replacement.[45]

I wrote in *Pixels and Place* about virtual reality as a great tool for increasing empathy in journalism and other storytelling, but the adoption of mixed reality into the mainstream has come a long way since then.

For example, the Weather Channel introduced a feature that demonstrates the effects of tornados through a mixed reality simulation by having a virtual tornado "trash" their own studio. While Jim Cantore, the anchor perhaps most known for his appearance in a place being synonymous with disastrous weather conditions, explains and provides information about tornado safety, a virtual electrical pole "falls into" the studio, a car is "blown in," and more. It's a sensationalist but educational play that helps people understand extreme weather and further establishes the Weather Channel as the experts on it.

A still from the Weather Channel virtual tornado video, via YouTube.com

You can read more about those opportunities in Mixed Reality for Storytelling and Empathy.

In my surveys asking people to define humans and the human experience, one of the responses I sometimes get back is "flawed" or "limited," and while that is undoubtedly true, we have ahead of us a great many tools to help us overcome some of those limitations. With the right tools, it might almost feel as if we know more, forget less, connect with people more easily, live healthier lives, avoid major catastrophes, and enjoy the world around us more fully. That is one possible set of outcomes, if we make the right decisions.

Meaningful Mobility

What will increasing amounts of data, technology, and tools mean for mobility, for transportation, and for travel?

We need to decide when we talk about autonomous cars: Whose autonomy are we talking about? Because if our mobility depends on machines we don't own and don't directly control, we are making a tradeoff. It may be a worthwhile tradeoff, it may even be an exciting tradeoff, but it's a tradeoff and we should acknowledge it.

We hear a lot about self-driving cars, but an area that gets less press and a lot of investment is trucking and logistics, where fleets of self-driving trucks could transform the industry—and wipe out waves of human jobs.

It's easy to understand the business case from a logistics point of view. Human truckers are limited to working sixty hours per week and must take periodic breaks[46], but in theory, a self-driving truck could operate nearly any of the remaining twenty-four hours a day, seven days a week that it's not being loaded or unloaded or undergoing repair.

Of course, the conditions and pay for long-haul truck driving have been in need of disruption for the good of humanity, anyway: One expert's term for the working conditions is "sweatshops on wheels[47]." Still, the potential job disruption is immense, with a reported 1.8 million truck-driving jobs[48] in the United States alone. Once again, we don't yet know the full impacts the eventual loss or redistribution of those jobs will have on individuals, society, and the economy overall.

In October 2016, a self-driving truck carrying a load of beer completed a 120-mile trip in Colorado from Fort Collins through downtown Denver to Colorado Springs[49]. The operation was controlled by self-driving technology company Otto, which was acquired by Uber for an estimated $680 million[50]. (That acquisition figure may have worked out differently in practice, though, as a result of Otto's former CEO being subsequently fired after having been accused of stealing company secrets from Google, where he had previously worked.[51])

Meanwhile, it is fair to say that the potential benefits to human experience include faster, more efficient distribution of goods and the convenience of being able to get something from one side of the continent to the other more quickly and presumably more cheaply. Cross-country moves, for example, would be totally different if people who didn't normally drive a twelve-thousand-pound truck didn't feel compelled to make harrowing attempts to drive one as a rental.

Suffice to say, there are big investments and big stakes in the automation of trucking, and we are only seeing the beginning of what's to come.

Where the broader industry of self-driving vehicles is concerned, the advances are accelerating. Those advances come with the need to prove the concept in as close to real situations as possible, so since Detroit has long been known as Motor City, the American home to car manufacturing, it makes sense that it is now home to an entire city made just for testing self-driving cars. Mcity is a thirty-two-acre mock-up city and test site on the University of Michigan campus in nearby Ann Arbor[52]. It contains about sixteen acres of roads and traffic infrastructure to create driving scenarios like crosswalks, bike lanes, roundabouts, and more.

Transportation is one of those areas of emerging technology that really makes the value of both/and integrated solutions more clear. In other words, should we be investing in autonomous vehicles or smarter, data-connected public transit, so that, among other benefits, riders have real-time information on when the next bus or train is coming and can map out their routes reliably? Both/and. Public transit serves the greater good at scale, but there are certainly use cases for both.

Of course the needs are different for people who are disabled, elderly, or injured. They may need elevators at subway stations, an easy step-up into a car, and highly reliable schedules for pickup and drop-off or else they may be at risk, for example, with exposure to the elements.

And while those are *necessary* features for some people, don't those sound like *desirable* features for almost everyone?

As we think about what kind of mobility solutions help the disabled and the elderly, for example, we often find solutions for people with occasional needs for individual accommodation. As we work to try to make the lives of more people better through the design of products and services, we will find that whatever makes some people's lives better may also improve the lives of greater numbers of people without these needs as well.

When I was in college, I heard a comedian who was in a wheelchair make a joke about how *of course* everyone wants to use the handicapped bathroom. (I wish I knew or could remember his name to give him credit. He was funny.) The upshot was: If you design for accessibility and for inclusivity, you are often designing a superior, more comfortable experience across all users of the service or product anyway.

Clearly, what is possible with technology-assisted business models is possible at scales not seen without them. You can see this in the rollout of dockless bike and scooter sharing programs. Ofo, for example, poured thousands of bikes into the Dallas market[53] using the "ask forgiveness, not permission" model embraced by Uber nearly ten years prior, and it backfired when the city council voted for restrictions that caused the company to decide to leave the market. (Full disclosure: I initially consulted with ofo in advance of their expansion into any US markets, but I didn't recommend this approach.)

Bikes as a whole are keys to greater equality. Bikes can help level access in poor neighborhoods. With bikes, people can commute to schools and jobs more reliably than with public transit and less expensively than with a car. Some activists advocate a concept known as bicycle equity:

> "To achieve it, cities are trying a number of things: steeply
> discounted memberships for food stamp recipients; bike-
> riding classes; pay stations that accept cash; and

recruiting riders from underserved neighborhoods. Bike equity sounds like a buzzword, but research shows it has its advantages: Bike sharing can bring disadvantaged communities a reliable—and healthy—alternative to mass transit, according to a June [2017] report by Portland State University in Oregon."
— http://www.governing.com/topics/urban/sl-bike-lane-equity-equality-income.html, referencing the study called "Evaluating Efforts to Improve the Equity of Bike Share Systems" by Nathan McNeil, John MacArthur, and Jennifer Dill, all of Portland State University

The tools that are now and soon becoming available to us stand to increase our mobility and freedom like never before—as long as we develop them with an eye toward human empowerment, greater quality of life, and the best futures for the most people.

Where Wearables Can Lead Us

Wearables have such interesting potential, and we have only begun to explore and experiment with them in any kind of mainstream sense. That certainly seems poised to change, though. In their Worldwide Quarterly Wearable Device Tracker report, the International Data Corporation (IDC) forecasts 240.1 million wearable devices will be shipped by 2021[54], and that's up from 104.3 million in 2016. A report from Juniper Research predicts that spend on wearable advertising will reach $68.7 million by 2019.[55]

Ask most people what they think of when they think of wearable technology, and their first response is to think about fitness trackers like FitBit. Some may think of Google Glass, and some may think of smart watches like Apple Watch. But as of 2018, that's largely the extent of what has made a splash on the mainstream market. Google

Glass may have been simply ahead of its time, though: Wearable eye accessories that integrate augmented reality seem like sure winners at some point in the not-too-distant future.

Voice integration with wearables is definitely picking up: Apple's $159 EarPods turned out to be a wildly popular accessory, and although Apple doesn't disclose their sales figures for the device specifically, analysts have forecast that by the end of 2018 Apple may have sold 26–30 million of them[56]. The rise of EarPods may be partly benefiting from the overall rise of audio and voice interaction as a general trend, and partly to thank for it. The next section, A Natural Shift to Audio and Voice, explores that macro trend further.

What else could be coming in the world of wearable technology? Smart fabrics and fashion technology represent an opportunity that's only begun to be explored.

In 2015 Google and Levi's announced their joint smart clothing project, the Project Jacquard platform. Their first available garment came in 2017, a $350 denim jacket aimed at bicycle commuters with integrated Bluetooth that can control music, get directions, or screen phone calls.[57]

Beyond fitness tracking and proactive health monitoring, wearables have huge potential in medical technology. MarketsandMarkets forecasts the global market for medical wearable devices to reach $12.1 billion by 2021[58]. Such devices include bracelets to patches to implantable devices, and the vast array of data they collect can revolutionize clinical trials: Researchers stand to find new links[59], as the wearables can monitor sleep, heart rate, physical activity, and other biometric information that can be correlated with other data to find patterns and insights to lead to innovative treatments.

The drawbacks have to do with security and regulatory limitations like HIPAA, but the upside seems significant enough to overcome the challenges.

Of course VR goggles, glasses, and headsets are already a popular category of wearable technology, and games and entertainment for VR seem poised to keep growing. But expect to see more uses in professional training, such as medicine.

New technology can augment the experience for prescriptions and reduce simulation sickness[60] including headaches and nausea by working with the responses of the human eye so that the optics can adjust automatically. Previous models of VR goggles have been challenging for users who wear prescription glasses, but this innovation should make that easier.

In fact, another VR innovation may lead the way toward auto-focusing corrective lenses for human eyes[61].

Few of the categories of emerging technology seem to make as clear a case for the integrative power of humans and technology as wearables. We seem to understand intuitively the benefit we get from immersive experiences and ever-present data. While implanted devices are still a bridge too far for many people, wearables are the closest link to being one with the data we generate, and to benefiting from that integration in real time.

A Natural Shift to Audio and Voice

A keyboard is an arbitrary interface; typing doesn't come naturally to humans. But it's instinct for us to interact through listening and with our voice.

One of the most transformational changes happening in the 2010s to 2020s is the shift from predominantly text- and touch-based interfaces to voice interfaces.

Just as mobile devices removed the limitation of being tethered to a desk for all connected needs, voice interactions remove the limitation of being in front of a screen. This makes voice the ideal platform for car interfaces, both in terms of interacting with the car's own feature set and in terms of operating a set of connected options such as connecting a phone through Bluetooth.

Some of the opportunity becoming available rides the coattails of the dominant marketplace trends, such as the huge swell of interest in smart audio devices. Smart speakers are already growing fast as an installed base and are widely forecast to be a huge category, with one forecast showing them with an installed base of 225 million units by 2020.[62]

The growth of this technology also accounts for the popularity of earbuds such as the Apple EarPods that have voice control capabilities, freeing up the person who wears them to operate nearly as normal while listening to music or a podcast, receiving calls, interacting with a virtual assistant, hearing notifications of updates to social media, and so on.

Our growing reliance on smartphones and their touchscreens and text keyboards over the first few decades of the twenty-first century has come with a safety cost: People text and drive, and people die as a result. And while initial studies have suggested that voice texting while driving is no safer than type-texting[63], part of what makes it dangerous is that a person might feel the need to look at the phone—and away from the road—to initiate the voice transcription feature and look again to see if their message was transcribed correctly. So smoother interfaces for initiating voice features, better integration into car controls and heads-up displays, and other design features may yet make voice texting just as safe as conversing with another passenger. (Although that also invites risk: Certain kinds of passenger interactions have also been linked with motorist accidents[64]. Basically, if you want to be safe, just drive alone and keep your eyes on the road.)

Of course the significance of all of that is due to shift as transportation with autonomous vehicles becomes more commonplace.

In the meantime, in most contexts, you're still reasonably safe consuming passive experiences, such as listening to music, an audiobook, or a podcast.

Speaking of which, while all of this smart earbud and speaker growth has been happening, there has also been substantial growth in the availability and popularity of podcasts: Apple reported in early 2018 that it hosts over 525,000 active shows, with more than 18.5 million episodes available, and the service has passed fifty billion all-time episode downloads and streams[65]. Just as with the shift in the TV and movies category, people are freeing themselves from traditional broadcasts and asserting control over what they listen to and when. For publishers and broadcasters this represents a major disruption in business as usual, but significant opportunity to integrate with emerging environments and contexts.

Beyond the audio content people consume, wearable audio devices, often called "hearables," include an emerging category of smart hearing enhancement devices—basically, souped-up hearing aids. In time they'll get better and better at amplifying the sounds a person wants to hear while filtering out the rest, incorporating some of the functionality of voice UI and voice-based assistants. Smart audio can also make use of directional sound—in other words, which way is your head pointed as you speak—which can become part of a context mesh that allows smarter, more responsive interactions. The former head of audio engineering at Doppler, Gints Klimanis, who was working on a hearable device before being hired away by another tech giant, put it this way: "Ultimately, the idea is to steal time from the smartphone."[66]

In addition, a wearable audio device could easily add biometrics data and gauge your health at an emotional level, not to mention have some indication of what you're thinking about.

As Peter Burrows noted in a *Fast Company* article about "hearables," "At this rate, it won't be long before Amazon can send ads for Robitussin when it hears you cough."

The human augmentation possibilities go beyond smart audio.

In 2016 Facebook introduced a feature that uses AI including image recognition to offer descriptions of the contents of photos so that someone who is blind or has a visual impairment can "see" what's in the photo.[67] Certainly the ability to parse the contents of photos being added to a social network might offer benefits to the company, too, in helping them understand trends and intent, allowing them to create even more compelling experiences and offers.

You have to think about how your product or service offering aligns with a world where people interact through voice command and conversation with machines, whether that conversation takes place in text or out loud.

See also Machine Learning, Deep Learning, Conversational AI, Natural Language Processing for clarification on some of the technology behind deploying these platforms, and Human Imitation by Machines for a discussion of the ethics of designing a machine-based interaction so that it is convincingly humanlike.

Chatbots and Other Conversational Interfaces

❊ ❊ ❊

Not all chat interactions are though voice, though. Sometimes a text-based/screen-based interaction makes more sense for how the person is likely to interact with it. Many websites have used integrated chat interfaces for a while; they're just getting more sophisticated all the time. See Should a Bot Have to Tell You It's a Bot for a further exploration of how this can work, as well as ethical considerations.

A whole category of therapy apps has emerged, such as Woebot, which offers a platform for people to "talk" through their feelings, track their moods, and use tools and exercises to manage their mental health. Clearly, people are willing to use it: According to the app's website, more than two million messages per week pass over the platform from across more than 120 countries[68]. Or there's Wysa, an app described as an "AI life coach" that helps users track their emotional states, their thoughts, and their sleep patterns, and boasts more than four hundred thousand users[69].

If it seems odd to imagine chatting with a bot about your deepest thoughts and feelings, imagine how many people refrain from talking about those thoughts and feelings because they feel they can't open up with anyone. The sense of anonymity that comes with a machine-based interaction may be exactly what helps people feel free to open up.

Beyond individual chat-based apps, there are messaging platforms, such as Facebook's Messenger platform, for which companies can build a custom bot app for commerce, bookings, directory searches, or other types of interactions suited to that environment.

CHAPTER 23

Measuring the Unmeasurable: Strategy and Data Modeling for Meaningful Experiences

YOU'VE PROBABLY HAD THAT MOMENT when you felt a deep sense of significance: looking at the horizon above the ocean, staring at the stars, holding a newborn baby. These moments of cosmic wonder help us forget time, take us out of the place we're in, and make us simultaneously aware of our mortality and connected to the vastness of all living things.

So if that kind of experience transcends time and place, how can we possibly measure it?

It's true that we cannot measure meaningfulness—although if we could, it might be helpful to think of these types of transcendent experiences as pegging the upper end of the scale. And most of us can well envision experiences at the low end of the scale: monotonous and routine tasks, actions that seem nonsensical to us but which we're obligated for one reason or another to fulfill. That at least gives us a senseof a range, and if that range can be felt through lived experience, it can be approximated in some kind of measurable objectives.

Of course, most of what we're trying to achieve on behalf of a business or entity will fall well short of the transcendent high end of our scale. But if we can understand the nature of those feelings—connectedness, purpose, sensory awareness, and so on—we can consider how to measure what approximates them, and to improve our efforts to maximize meaningfulness in the experiences we create.

We can find proxies for meaningfulness. Memorable experiences, for example, are a reasonable proxy for meaningful experiences, and that might be easier to test or measure.

Maybe right now the closest you can get as a company to measuring the meaning of the experiences you create for the human who has decided to be your customer is asking whether they liked the product or service, whether they would recommend it to others, or whether they would buy again. These are starting points.

From there, we can explore what it means for our interactions when we have created a meaningful experience, and we may hypothesize what may be meaningful for the humans who buy from us. If you're Apple and you're selling iPhones, you may create an ad campaign that shows amazing photos with the caption "Shot on an iPhone." As many photographers say, the best camera is the one you have with you, and the iPhone campaign is alluding to the universal experience of witnessing something beautiful and wanting to capture it in the best way possible. That's arguably a meaningful message because it taps into an intuitive understanding of a meaningful experience.

In any case, the great driver of all kinds of business and experiences now and for the foreseeable future is data. Everything is about the measuring of everything, the tracking of everything, and putting it all in accessible, retrievable, calculable formats that we can draw from and mix and match and remaster for great insights. And sometimes that even works.

But it is also important for us to remember that the vast majority of that data is about humans: it measures real people and our interests, our motivations, our preferences, our movements, our needs. I often say "analytics are people." I encourage my clients to start with empathy. We know companies are going to use customer data, so I want to equip them with frameworks for doing it ethically, mindfully, and meaningfully. We know companies will collect customer data and use it to sell products and services; we can help them do it in a way that puts the human in the perspective.

Think about the motivations and needs of the people you're trying to do business with. It is easier to craft a human-centric data model when you start trying to understand how the needs and desires of the person you're doing business with align with the objectives of the company.

A disciplined focus on customer experience within an iterative process of improvement yields profit.

There's a reason we use the term *visitor* to refer to people who browse our websites: They are our guests. If you've hosted parties, you know that the best way to ensure people have a great perception of the party is to pay attention to the details that make it a good experience. The details need not be extravagant; they just have to be relevant and appropriate to the situation. In the same way, your digital efforts can perform quite effectively without extravagant features, necessarily; you just need to pay attention to the details that make your guests feel like telling their friends what a great experience it was.

People have often used the expression "data is the new oil" to highlight the value of data to business, and how it needs refinement to realize its full potential. But the oil is not just data in the abstract; we *are* the data. When I say that "analytics are people," I mean the data businesses collect is by and large made up of the transactions and interactions of real people. So, actually, we are the oil.

It couldn't be more important that we let that sink in as we go forward.

How Data Shapes Experiences

As humans, we need to understand how our experiences shape the data we generate in the world, and in turn how our data shapes our experiences.

I often talk about the "data trail," and experiences that adapt, expand, retract, and reshape around each of us based on the data we generate as we move through the world.

But the scope of the data trail and the full implications of it to us individually and collectively go well beyond what many people think about.

For example, as a starting point, most of us realize that our purchase data shapes the offers and coupons we receive. So far so good.

We may also realize that our financial data shapes our credit score. So does our housing history, home ownership records, and other investment and credit history, which in turn shape further financial and other opportunities we may have — or not have.

Experiences may also be shaped by

- Your driving record
- Your health records, which can also affect your insurance, which in turn shapes your opportunities for medical care
- Your criminal record
- Your voting data
- Your census data
- Your demographic profile
- Your online browsing history
- Your tracked visits to certain physical retailers
- Your social media interactions, the people you're connected with, the posts and activities you've "liked" and viewed, and so on

Many of these are one-to-one, cause-and-effect types of relationships. But there are amplifying network effects of the cumulative access to big data.

When you browse social networks, you can be pinpointed and retargeted across devices. And if you are browsing from your phone, your smartphone can even be targeted directly with offers and messages including location-specific ones.

The aggregate of data that includes information about you can be compiled many times over by many types of services, if certain identifiable characteristics are stripped out. But sometimes those aren't needed; lookalikes and other techniques can be used to come close to hyper-segmenting people and targeting them for customized and personalized offers.

In addition, the information we are exposed to varies depending on many factors. Content algorithms and product recommendation algorithms make snap determinations for us about the optimal catalog highlights, page layouts, featured articles, and more. Our experiences using everything from search engines to on-demand entertainment sites are largely personalized and optimized. Algorithms interact with other algorithms to create experiences for us. Increasingly, it's algorithms all the way down.

Not all of this is necessarily scary, and even what tends toward the invasive isn't all equally threatening. You may find yourself getting better, more useful offers and discounts for brands you like, and you may discover new products you like. You may reconnect with people you have lost track of. You may discover new music and movies you enjoy. You may find more relevant information and resources. Any of those experiences are generally positive. But what's not good is that so few people have sufficient understanding of all that is happening behind the scenes through connected systems with nearly everything they do, nearly everything they buy, and nearly everywhere they go, and the legitimate risk all of that *does* carry.

Because beyond those basics, the very real broader implications that are currently or potentially shaping people's opportunities pose threats to individual liberties and social justice.

When people's insurance costs change or their options become limited based on big data and profiling, there's a very real possibility that unfair discrimination will take place.[70]

When law enforcement relies on predictive data based on tracking that may already contain bias within it, it can lead to disproportionate policing of areas where wealth inequality and systemic injustices already exist.[71]

Where targeted marketing facilitates racism because certain housing options aren't being shown to people of color[72] while other more predatory options are[73], there's a problem with the entire model.

And facial recognition, which people are increasingly using for authentication—allowing you access to your locked phone, for example, or perhaps your bank account—can also be used at scale in ways that compete with human interests, such as by law enforcement to identify suspects, even if the results aren't always accurate. (The CEO of Axon, the largest supplier of body cameras in the United States, says he doesn't think facial recognition results are accurate enough yet[74].) Or when used to identify people participating in a political protest[75].

There's more about some of those issues in the section on Chapter 28 - Ethics at Scale.

In the meantime, it behooves people to be aware *and* it behooves companies to be proactive and thoughtful about this—both because the alignment with human interests will serve them well as time goes on, and because as new legislation is introduced, such as GDPR in Europe and other emerging privacy measures elsewhere, companies don't want to have to backpedal and play catch-up with compliance.

Where the rubber meets the road shapes the future possibilities of business and allows us to create more meaningful experiences. So how does data figure into that? More and more, data is being used adaptively to inform product recommendations, behavioral options, and even availability of product customizations. So next we'll get into how to build a company culture that works effectively and respectively with data.

Developing Organizational Agility with Data

Now that we understand a bit more about how we as humans generate data and how that data is shaping our experiences, we can turn to thinking about how to build effective data models and culture within our companies to use data effectively and respectfully. Much is made of the idea of "data-driven" business, "data-driven" marketing, "data-driven" culture, and "data-driven" decision-making, but I'm not a fan of that term. If anything, "data-driven" is what human experiences are largely becoming, and that's why the businesses creating those experiences must be thinking more holistically and integratively. Data is rarely what should be "driving" decisions or culture; instead data should be *informing* decision-making. That may sound like a picky distinction, but nuance matters in how we understand meaning, and the larger point is this: *Purpose* should be driving culture.

Data is rarely what should be driving decisions or culture; purpose should be driving culture.

That said, organizational data must be richly modeled and easily accessible, and the organization must have a data-ready mindset when it comes to decision-making. Organizational agility is a key attribute in adopting this more purpose-driven, human-centric, data-informed Tech Humanist approach, but agility with data is especially important.

What does it mean to have agility with data?

We need to use data to model the business for insights and to gain effectiveness. Where the data models the business and models the most meaningful parts of the business—those parts, those interactions, those decision points where changes can lead to make or break financial outcomes, customer success or failure, etc.

Many leaders believe data and analytics are the biggest drivers of change right now. Data is being used to track all kinds of behavioral intent, proximity information, relational information, brand affinities, and so on. That's mostly just referring to company transactional data, but there's also the power of big data, characterized by its velocity, variety, and volume (and more recently, people have begun to add "veracity") that can be correlated dimensionally with other data sets. And open data, meaning data sets that have been made available for sharing and repurposing.

Could a new approach to data transform your company or organization?

Are there either open data sets you may be able to integrate, or even perhaps data sets of your own you can publish and share for the sake of shared progress in solving a public problem?

The British newspaper the *Guardian* has made its raw data with two million content items dating back to 1999 available for reuse in an open API.[76] Atlas Van Lines uses publicly available US census bureau information[77] that could help inform decisions related to logistics, marketing, and a wide variety of operations.

Data democratization in business means all departments have

access to customer data. Data in many organizations has been "owned" by the business intelligence (BI) unit or the broader IT departments, and someone in, say, marketing, HR, or finance might have had to log a request to have a developer access it and generate a spreadsheet. The access to organizational data through enterprise analytics platforms and self-service BI platforms has democratized access to knowledge. This is important to allow knowledge to be shared, to allow the organization to become smarter, more connected, and less siloed.

Everyone in the company can become data literate enough to serve many of their own needs, as discussed in the Developing Organizational Agility with Data section. Data literacy also develops employees' appreciation for the role of data in decision-making and increases the likelihood that their own decisions will be informed by data.

A more integrative view of data that gives directional insight and adds value for all stakeholders is healthy.

Could data help your company make more closely aligned decisions? Could it incentivize the right kind of teamwork that leads to the kinds of innovations you need?

How can you cultivate a data-agile organizational mindset?

It takes some practice to know where data tells enough of a story, and where human insights are needed.

There is value in being able to explain what a data pattern suggests, but sometimes you can't, and sometimes you just need to act on what the data tells you. (See also Start with Empathy, Scale Through Meaning and the discussion there on finding a narrative in data analytics.)

Of course, it helps to understand when instinct is relevant, too. After all, as a business leader you are often faced with decisions to make with seemingly no data and change you can't control (see also Bigger Than "Digital": Transforming to Agility). That's why, as often as you have the luxury, you should cultivate a bias toward consulting data when making decisions. And then a discipline to respond to what the data shows. To iterate, to adapt, and ultimately to evolve based on what you learn.

Defining a Meaningful Data Model

Don't be intimidated by the idea of data models.

Imagine you're a teacher with a classroom full of small kids. Let's say you wanted to give an award to the kids who were the most well-behaved, the best students, etc.

You might want to keep track of who shows up every day, who arrives on time, and who gets there late. You'll probably want to keep track of the grades they get.

Whatever adds meaningfully to the insight you have about each student, without leading you into faulty decision-making.

It's all too easy to default to the same measures every business uses: profit, revenue, growth, etc.

What you measure helps you determine what efforts to optimize and maximize, what efforts to adapt or transform.

If you put your purpose articulation on one end and profit on the other, and you filled in the metrics and strategic components in between, you might actually have a pretty clear starting point of what a meaningful data model looks like for your organization.

The only way to get to meaningful measures is to align data and tech with strategy.

Draw up a data model that spans the whole organization, from the earliest points where humans begin interacting with the system. Be intentional and thoughtful about it so that you track the right measures. Be aware that you only rarely get lucky enough to be able to reconstruct some kind of historical data set or data trail for a metric that you didn't intentionally set out to track, so it's worthwhile to periodically review what you're tracking and what you need to adjust so you're tracking meaningful, useful data points.

When you're looking for places to measure, consider where handoffs happen, where time passes between steps, where value is added, where complexity exists, and where decisions have to be made. Organizations vary from one another, and the value in each one is some combined magic of what is measurable with what is not measurable. But again, even what isn't directly measurable often has a proxy in some form, so just do your best to draw out what's unique and valuable as you build your data model.

Every part of the organization should be able to measure something that meaningfully contributes to the strategic purpose and the larger goals.

Netflix provided me with a wonderful example of this fairly early in my career. As I wrote in a short e-book about my time working at Netflix called *Lessons from Los Gatos*:

> **"Keep the entire company focused on moving a single key metric that really matters.**
>
> Ours was customer-focused and most early-stage companies will want theirs to be, too. We wanted to have one million active subscribers to the service by July of that year. You can choose a different 'most important metric' as time goes by and you hit your goals, and the business needs shift and grow. But having everyone making daily decisions based on knowing that one top-level goal ensures you will have the best chance of hitting it.
>
> **Empower your department heads to determine a relevant key metric for their area of focus that influences the company's key metric.**
>
> Not only does this help grow the management capabilities of every area in the company, it helps everyone think through how their work is accountable for hitting or missing the big number. As the manager of the content group, I was given latitude to understand and determine

what my department's key metric would be. I chose content completeness, understanding that a rigorous attention to thorough metadata would be meaningful if we wanted customers to navigate organically to the deepest recesses of the content library so they'd appreciate the richness of their rental options and remain customers longer. We determined a standard set of metadata we wanted complete for all titles in the catalog, and based on this matrix, when we started, the catalog was 3% complete. Within a few months, we were at 97% completion, all while improving the efficiency of our content entry and while working on other new projects. It was a small thing in the grand scheme of things, but my team was proud of it."[78]

What data can you capture throughout the business that will answer questions about the brand, culture, and purpose and provide further insight?

Modeling Relevance and Empathy for Scale

What works in small scale doesn't always hold true writ large.

Retargeting can be effective, for example, but without a thoughtful approach, it can quickly get silly.

If I were to buy a refrigerator, I'd hope it would be a long time before I'd need to see more ads for refrigerators. Yet too often that's the way retargeting is set up: as if our past browsing and purchase behaviors are absolute predictors of our future needs, when very often the circumstances evolve and the context changes, and the model doesn't allow for that.

So even something as seemingly benign as relevance can go too far.

A Tech Humanist assessment of analytics might be that the goal of any kind of analytics that are predominantly reactive would be to facilitate adaptation, and that the goals of any kind of predictive analytics would be to model empathy.

Recognizing Symptoms of Non-Meaningful Experiences

Many different metrics and symptoms could indicate in your particular business that you're not creating a differentiated enough brand, a clear enough offering, and a meaningful enough experience.

For example:
- High churn
- Having to spend a lot of money to acquire new customers
- Low rate of trial to paid user adoption

These metrics are only directional indicators. If you try too hard to solve for one particular metric, you risk upsetting the delicate balance of the ecosystem. The Tech Humanist approach is to look at these metrics as invitations to consider a more holistic approach to addressing them and improving the experience.

Fostering an Organization-Wide Mindset for Metrics

In a previous work life, I worked for Magazines.com and led their customer experience and product development efforts. It was a great role that gave me autonomy to explore a great many ideas about how to improve both the company's bottom line and the experience that the customer would have with our website and our brand.

But taking the wisdom Jim Collins wrote about in *Good to Great* to heart, I began to think about how to dimensionalize our profit measurement in ways that would be more enlightening. So instead of focusing on profit as a whole, I began to look at profit per subscription, which meant digging deeper into analytics to find what was happening beyond a purchase level and aligning the data to show me for each subscription how profitably we had conducted the whole transaction.

Then I thought, since I want this to be about the customer, it should be profit per *subscriber*, not per subscription. Again, that meant going beyond the individual purchase and looking at a customer's history through their interactions with us, and trying to understand what insights we might gain about acquisition, engagement, and retention for different sets of subscribers based on their longevity as a customer, based on the category of magazine they subscribed to, based on whether they gifted subscriptions or not, and so on.

Then it dawned on me that since we knew that our company's success was dependent upon renewals for subscriptions, and since a renewing customer was a reasonable proxy, at least initially, for a satisfied customer, we should really be tracking profit for renewing subscribers.

This realization led to the development of a whole set of hybrid metrics that gave me and my team incredible insights and instincts about how to engage with different sets of customers effectively, what kind of features to provide, and what might keep them around longer. The data modeling insight also led to brand insight about how to enrich the way we talked about the ease and appeal of renewal.

In the end, through these and other projects and programs, I helped usher in a nine-million-dollar impact in one year by improving customer retention—by recognizing an opportunity to improve the renewals process—and our team increased overall site conversion rates by 40 percent YOY.

All of this holistic thinking, when put in practice, really does lead to success by any traditional measure.

It has to be organizational; you have to share a company mindset for metrics.

How will we measure this? We can look for compound and combined metrics that mean more and reflect company priorities more than simple metrics. Not just profit, but profit per X.

With the right metric, usually a hybrid metric of some sort, you can keep the focus on both profit and the person who is interacting with the company.

Aligning Incentives and Measuring Meaningful Results

While it's healthy to hold a department leader accountable for their team's performance, it's also tempting to reduce the tendency toward transparency if there is punishment for failing to achieve outcomes despite smart strategy, sensible experiments, and strong efforts.

So it's important, too, to align incentives across the organization, so that what is measured is measured honestly, and everyone is incentivized to achieve the same outcomes.

A profit motive tends to be pushed up the hierarchical ladder (valued) when justifying/rationalizing decisions, while customer value motive tends to be pushed down the ladder (devalued). Is there another/better way? Can we share incentives?

Everyone should be aligned on two things: achieving the company purpose and making the human experience better. Beyond that, departmental metrics should lead to clarity about where opportunities exist to tighten and tune those efforts.

The classic example is a sales organization based on commission incentives, where the salespeople are incentivized to sell at nearly any cost, sometimes leading to making promises that are difficult for the rest of the company to fulfill—i.e., delivery dates for software features that can't be met, or product demand that exceeds the operational pipeline. Some would say these are good problems to have, but they're still misalignment; and misalignment leads to internal struggles, mistrust, and a general lack of focus on the human the company is trying to serve.

Make sure your efforts to be meaningful are not measured in meaningless terms. Profit may be too narrow a viewpoint for a longer-term play on experience, for example. If an effort brings your organization into better alignment, the results should be measurable across the organization but may be subtle. A 2 percent lift in performance across every department will certainly improve the bottom line eventually, but it may be hard to trace back to an internal campaign to align team language around the customer.

So you'll need some way to gauge success that looks more closely at the shorter-term impacts, as well as some way to determine if programs are putting your company on the right track longer term.

Cultivating a Culture of Data Literacy

If the most valuable asset in business is data—and it also happens to be one asset that's deeply personal because every single one of us is affected by every other business's data-related practices—then every business needs to develop sophisticated practices about gathering data and protecting it.

It is important to promote data analysis literacy throughout the company: how to read insights from data, analytics, and metrics. Challenge your organization to become more agile with data, while also being more protective of it.

Years ago I was leading customer experience for an e-commerce website and we had just invested in a testing platform. I wasted no time getting my hands dirty. I had the first test running on the home page in a day.

Over the next few months, my team and I tested all kinds of things. I was still in play-with-it mode of on-site testing, but there was one gap in the numbers we couldn't seem to move. It was the number of people who moved from the cart page to the checkout page.

We tried designing it differently. We tried a red button, we tried a blue button; we tried rounded corners, we tried square corners; we tried two columns, we tried one column.

On something of a whim, I toyed with moving the "proceed to checkout" button down ten pixels, and that one move generated a 12 percent lift in clicks through the page.

What that taught me is that sometimes the best rationale doesn't play out like you think it will, and sometimes something that has very little rational explanation works best. Which is why you need data.

When conducting user research, people offered input about what they would want that didn't test out to be true. Sometimes things that people say they want aren't actually what perform best. Which is why you need data.

It can sometimes be helpful to differentiate between data, metrics, and analytics, so my reductive definitions would be something like: *Data* is the more inclusive term that includes the logging of just about any transactional information in any system; *metrics* are the specific measurements you evaluate, and hopefully choose with intention; *analytics* generally refers more to systems or platforms of data collection, or the discipline of performing that analysis.

Data should be well labelled, well sourced, appropriately structured, and clean. Be sure your organization is practicing good data hygiene. If you don't know where the data came from or how reliable it is, it's probably best not only *not* to use it but also to purge it from your data repositories or wall it off, in a manner of speaking. Do what you have to do to make sure that flawed, incomplete, erroneous, or unethically sourced data doesn't end up being part of your queries or your organizational decision-making.

Measuring, Optimizing, and Closing the Loop

You're a lot more likely to get meaningful insights out of meaningful measurements than measurements that are default or haphazard. Every once in a while you might stumble onto a gem of an insight in the data you're tracking by default, but those insights are a lot more likely to happen if you develop a strategy and discipline for modeling what matters into your numbers.

You strategize, you measure, you experiment, you optimize, and you close the feedback loop. Make hypotheses, review the results, consider what you learn from them. Bring your learnings back into the organization. Share them widely. Make everyone smarter. Give everyone the power of knowledge that reinforces the purpose and value of what you are working on. Let everyone see the potential for collaborating to solve problems and improve as an organization.

When your purpose is represented in strategy that is

dimemsionalized in brand and culture and modeled through data and amplified through technology, everything you learn stands to come back to the top and feed back nuance about how that purpose aligns with what people in the marketplace need.

It may mean adjusting your goals, or how you have allocated resources.

It may even mean adjusting your articulation of purpose.

Closing the loop and learning from data is the Tech Humanist way of building a human-centric organization that is guided at every level by purpose, and successful in ways everyone can feel good about.

CHAPTER 24

Upgrade the Whole System: Digital Transformation, Purpose, Alignment, Future-Readiness

THE TECH HUMANIST FUTURE IS only achievable if business goals, which drive technology forward, are better aligned with what's best for humanity. This shouldn't be as hard as it is; after all, we're all human.

But somehow the pursuit of profit as an end unto itself has become a fixture of business thinking. And don't get me wrong: I enjoy making a profit. Far more than not making a profit. I enjoy having money. I find, and I don't think this is a very controversial opinion, that it's a more comfortable way to exist than, say, not having money.

But once you establish that it's nicer to have some money than not having money, what comes after that? Does it follow that we should put the money at the center of our pursuits? Of course not; no reasonable person would make that argument on a personal level. We are cautioned about the emptiness of seeking money without having a sense of personal fulfillment in our endeavors.

Somehow when it comes to business, it's expected that money will be the central measure, above and beyond all others. Even though we're all humans working within the company. (For now.) And even though money is a very misleading metric when it comes to how much good the business does, or how rewarding it is as an employer, or how productively it is contributing to a better world for the future.

Money doesn't even motivate all decision-making in most organizations; anyone who's ever worked more than a day in the average company knows emotions run high, personal preferences enter into decision-making, relationship dramas play out across the hierarchy, and political maneuvering is tantamount to survivorship.

We can address all of that. If we take the time to identify and align our objectives on an organizational level, we can better navigate personal and political dramas and dynamics and can work together to achieve a profitable outcome that fulfills us on a human level.

Digital Transformation Is Actually Bigger Than "Digital"

Machine-driven experiences are not new; they've been around in various industries for decades. We've had automated teller machines since the 1970s, and car manufacturers have been using robots on the line since the 1980s. The shift from humans doing a task to machines or robots or software or systems doing a task is not new.

So if we've been at this whole automation thing for a while, why is it suddenly such a hot topic?

Is it because of the emphasis on "digital transformation"? Well, sort of. But I think digital transformation is a bit of a misnomer.

We already mostly made a *digital* transformation the minute most of us started working in front of computers all day long in bits and bytes. Digital, the way we've thought about it for decades, is only about technology that's powered by chips and electronics. And that's only part of the story. What is more to the point, in terms of the major changes we're seeing corporately and culturally, is to talk about the *data* being generated, collected, and analyzed through our devices, appliances, accessories, and all kinds of other tools and resources.

What we're really talking about in business is a *data transformation,* a fundamental push toward data-informed decision-making, toward letting algorithms help optimize our business, toward connecting data end points in the organization, toward making our devices and displays and transactions "smart" and responsive and predictive.

Our businesses are throwing off data left and right, but most leaders feel they don't know how to use that data, yet they know they need to build systems to help them maximize the potential of what they're collecting. We know we need algorithms that help us optimize the operations, a connected understanding of one output and another output. The endpoints need to talk to each other; systems of smartness between them. That's happening whether the transactions originate in physical or digital space.

Pulling all of this data out of different parts of the organization and then combining it and centralizing it and decentralizing it and making it accessible across the organization to different stakeholders to make decisions based on it so that they can be more empowered to create more meaningful human experiences with it—now *that* takes transformation.

And of course, amid all this talk about digital transformation we're also talking about artificial intelligence, which is an umbrella term for a whole set of technologies. By that we mean machine learning, image recognition, cognitive computing, neural networks, deep learning, natural language processing, and all kinds of distributed and automated intelligence built on data and foundationally informed by the rules and logic we feed it.

But also, don't get me wrong: The "transformation" part definitely still applies, because it's also about change, about adaptation. About the ability to adapt to changing landscapes and market expectations, to keep up with the times, to scale. It's about agility with data.

What we call "digital transformation" is fundamentally about agility with data.

And that business data we're collecting and optimizing? Most of it is about people.

The data we collect in business—the data that passes through our systems — represents the needs and interests and motivations and desires of real people out there in the market: how they're doing business with you, their transactions and interactions and touchpoints with systems all along the way.

Business data, by and large, is about people.

The underlying story of this transformation to data is how you can align with people's inherent incentives and what they value and what they find meaningful.

That's really the core of this question, as we stand here in this moment, about to transform our businesses, about to automate like never before: What if we used all this data, automation, efficiency, and technology to achieve the best of what humanity is capable of? What if we used data and emerging tech to transform experiences around what makes humanity thrive?

Digitization Versus Digitalization Versus Digital Transformation

There's definitely something larger going on about the word *digital* and why it feels like it applies here in a new way. What does the "digital" in digital transformation and digital experience really refer to? Is digital more than a channel, more than a medium? In some contexts, is it also a culture? Heck, is it an *ethos*?

Even digital strategy is really data strategy, but only if you think about data in a big enough way.

Some analysts and pundits even use a range of terms to make the distinction between digitization versus digitalization versus digital transformation. Typically, digitization is about converting physical assets to digital; digitalization is about converting manual processes to digitally driven workflows; and digital transformation is about a full, integrated approach to a wholesale change in business processes and offerings based on the full capabilities of technology.

These may be fair and reasonable distinctions if they help you.

But one way or another, if your business is behind the curve on embracing digital assets and tools, it may be worthwhile to leapfrog into wholly transformed business. The scale and scope of the experiences being driven by machines are rapidly increasing, and the best way to set your company up for success is to get human-centric as soon as possible.

Bigger Than "Digital": Transforming to Agility

Nobody really wants transformation, per se. They want improvement. They want opportunities. They want obstacles removed from their paths. They want convenience, safety, assurances of their privacy even as they share personal data left and right. If they run a business, they want to reduce the risk of becoming irrelevant, of having upstart competitors emerge seemingly out of nowhere and wipe out their market share in a year.

But nobody wants to wake up one day transformed. That makes me think of a giant cockroach. Nobody wants to adjust and adapt everything they're doing in one fell swoop when change comes calling. No one wants to give up their habits, their tastes, their routines — not all at once.

And I mean inside or outside of business. No one welcomes decisions for which they feel they have insufficient data, and no one welcomes change beyond their control. But those are decisions business leaders need to make all the time, which is why it's so important to cultivate a habit of consulting data when it's available and the discipline to act when the data shows something that needs action. (See Developing Organizational Agility with Data for more on that.)

When we talk about digital transformation, we have to wonder what we're proposing to transform *from* and *to*.

It's less about digital than data; data is people; as for "transformation," it's not just business operations, but just about everything around us — most business models, most interactions.

Leaders struggle for a business rationale and strategy for a successful, scalable, future-ready digital transformation that doesn't lose sight of the human experience

Given all this, why is it important to focus on the human experience? Because it allows you to dimensionalize the aspects of the interaction that will make it compelling. It's a win-win.

Whatever happens within your organization, it's important to remember you can't simply transform one day and have a magically new company with a magically new product and magically new processes. The culture is an important part of the transformation, and everything has to be in alignment.

If digital transformation is largely about agility with data, and business data is largely about people, then our job in transforming our companies is to optimize what works best for people. And since we know that humans thrive on meaning, and we know that meaning in business strategy takes the shape of organizational purpose and alignment, we can look for ways to infuse purpose and alignment throughout the organization. Our companies will run more efficiently and everyone who interacts with the company, both inside and outside, if they share values with the company and the brand, will tend to be more motivated and more loyal.

Which means looking at every opportunity to make business more human.

Kill the Bureaucracy: It's Neither Human-Centric Nor Conducive to Transformation

As you think about how your company can innovate and transform, don't forget the power of simplification. Organizations codify their workflow into bureaucracies in attempt to scale and reproduce reliable results, but bureaucracies are not human-centric, and the work patterns they grow up around and protect tend to ossify without considering their changing contexts. So before you expend effort on transforming to model certain procedures in data or deploy technology to accelerate them, make sure those work processes are useful and meaningful. In other words, make sure they help people do good work.

If there are processes within your company that no longer apply to the way work is done or should be done, get rid of them.

I once worked with a company that, in one department, had an intake form that included a field for an arcane project tracking number that wasn't common knowledge. It seemed out of the blue and required some digging for people to complete. In digitizing this intake process, we began to ask about this tracking number and what it connected to. Turns out, it related to the preferences of an executive long since gone from the company and a tracking system long since replaced. The department's employees, when asked, always verbally told people to ignore that field. But that's *if* you thought to ask. Countless hours must have been wasted by employees all across the company who routinely wasted effort trying to figure out what their project's tracking number was before submitting this form — because no one in the department had ever bothered updating the form to remove the field.

Reducing needless bureaucracy will free people up to work the way the work really needs to be done — arguably even more so than automation, in many cases — and that can go a long way toward making the space to be creative and human-centric.

Systemwide Upgrades

If I were to ask you what the most ingenious product ever invented was, what would come to mind? The iPod, or perhaps the iPhone? Lipitor? The Toyota Corolla?

What about Amazon Prime? It's not what most people would think of as a "product," perhaps, but it is an offering the company makes, it is something customers pay for, and it is perhaps the most brilliant scheme ever designed.

Amazon introduced one-click ordering and trained us to feel friction about checkout. They introduced Prime and taught us to be wary of shipping costs. Studies have shown that when there are multiple sellers listed on Amazon for a product, people will sometimes even select the higher-priced option sold by Amazon with Prime instead of opting for a lower-priced option from a third-party seller.

(I've probably even done it myself.) The default two-day shipping is one possible factor; sometimes it's not cost but speed that drives that purchase.

True, Amazon Prime—and even Amazon as a whole—may not be the *best* example of a human-centric experience, but it's a great example of optimizing the business around what drives it—the "flywheel effect," to use *Good to Great*[79] language. It demonstrates a holistic approach to the organizational model and incentives that are worth taking note of, and looking for ways to emulate in more human-centric ways in other companies. With Amazon it's almost as if the experience *is* Prime; whatever you're buying is secondary. While a Tech Humanist review of the company's playbook may find plenty to critique, with Amazon's market capitalization at the trillion-dollar mark, the company's strategies have to merit a strategist's serious consideration for their successful scale alone. We just can't forget to view them through the Tech Humanist lens, as well. (And don't worry; we'll get to that. See Chapter 28 - Ethics at Scale and Don't Let Absurdity Scale for a more critical look at some of Amazon's problems with—you guessed it— scale.)

There are plenty of usability drawbacks on the core Amazon.com website experience. (I've consulted with clients who've mentioned to me in some way that they want to adopt some practice Amazon follows on its website, and I always tell them "no you don't." The quirks on Amazon.com are something those of us who shop there are used to. They can get away with it. You might not be able to.)

There's no easy way to get in touch with Amazon's customer service. They've pushed as much of the support as possible to FAQs and form-driven interaction. In exchange, they have a pretty lax return policy. I'm sure it costs them less to take a slight hit on returned merchandise and shipping in the name of long-term customer loyalty and lifetime value.

Whether Amazon Prime is an example of productizing your operational model or operationalizing your product may not matter. What matters is that businesses take a good look at the scale that can come from understanding what is causing friction for your customers and what your customers' incentives are, and developing integrative systems to address them.

It's also not necessarily a technology play, but it isn't *not* a technology play, either. In other words, it takes plenty of backend systems—from the systems that provide that first-level support to product catalog and content management to inventory management to warehousing, fulfillment, deployment, distribution, and supply chain management—to make Amazon Prime successful. Those technology decisions don't happen in a vacuum, and at the scale they're operating, improvements to any of them have substantial effect on both the customer experience and the bottom line.

Take another look at Netflix, for example, and their ability to look at streaming as a possible future and know it would still fulfill the purpose of providing entertainment options and that the experience of it would still be one of selection, recommendation, and subscription. The icing on the cake is that they invested in the Netflix prize to make sure their recommendation engine was as good as it could be.

And then came the pivot to original content—another alignment with purpose, and another question of human experience. But in this instance they were using the data they now had from years of streaming[80] to discern who watches what, how long, how much they binge, when they abandon, and so on, so they could create the kind of shows that would be the most satisfying (or you could say addictive). The big picture investments have paid off time and again, but in iterative, adaptive, evolutionary ways that only work if your organization is aligned with a central purpose and all of your decision-making is in sync.

What about Apple's pivots? Are there instructive patterns to follow or ponder there? Their purpose still relates to design and delight, and the experience of their customers still broadly relates to fandom and obsessive use.

Wherever you look among the most successful companies, you can find patterns, insights, and provocations. You can see where they have done well, as well as where they could have been more human-centric.

Understanding underlying objectives can lead to realizations of priorities that seem counterintuitive, too, like the importance to Tesla Inc. of investing research and development resources into more efficient energy storage. Is Tesla a car company or a battery company? They're not necessarily either one: At root, you could say they're about accelerating sustainable transportation. Many different mini-pivots along the way could make that happen.

An array of these tools could be used to consider and apply how to develop a Tech Humanist approach to strategy and operations, which will substantially inform the data and technology investments you need to make.

CHAPTER 25

Iterate as You Learn

YOU CAN MAKE A CASE for or against whether iteration is the way to innovation. Some will say it is not; that innovation comes from a more radical place. But introducing something truly new to the world and having it be a smashing success is rare. In most cases, even the most radically new idea may need tweaks or adjustments to resonate as clearly as possible. And when it comes to leading an organization from yesterday's processes to tomorrow's, radical innovation will often seem too risky.

And when change feels too risky, sometimes we just don't make it, even when we need to. Or we drag our feet, procrastinating until we can make it "perfect," when the reality is our first attempts probably won't be perfect. But if we can improve on them a little bit at a time, we can get something out sooner rather than later and see how it works. In start-up parlance, this is the Minimum Viable Product approach. In a more established company, it may mean launching an app with one important feature rather than five—such as a bank launching the ability to log in safely and check balances, but not yet, say, make remote deposits—but adding each of the remaining features in updates to the app if people's usage of the app supports the addition of those features.

So to get to a Tech Humanist place, you can embrace iteration perhaps not as the path to innovation, but as a part of innovation. Put your radically new idea into the world, see how it is received by the people you intend it for, and let their reactions — confusion, excitement, concern, indifference, etc. — inform what you do next with it.

An iterative approach is the closest thing in the business world to applying the scientific method: Develop a hypothesis, design an experiment to test it, and examine the results to determine if they validate or invalidate the hypothesis (or if more data might be needed). This approach isn't right for every decision, but it goes hand in hand with developing organizational agility with data and a culture of data literacy.

CHAPTER 26

Adapt: Navigating Change and Growing Meaningfully

As you lead your company through changing times, you need comprehensive approaches to managing change. We've already talked about iteration; now we're talking about adaptation, and in the next section we'll talk about evolution. These words sound similar, so how do they differ in the stages of the overall Tech Humanist approach to integrative business transformation? **Iteration** is about incremental change, repeated experiments to achieve breakthrough results or insights. **Adaptation** is setting yourself up for the organizational changes those insights lead you toward, improving internal processes, and making aligned partnerships. **Evolution** is about digging in and making deeper changes in your business model in response to culture, the competitive landscape, consumer demand, market trends, and so on.

Marketing—and to some extent, all of business—has always been about what Peter Drucker said: "to know and understand the customer." The rest of that quote is "so well the product fits him or her and sells itself," but you can take it one part at a time. The first part is about alignment; the second part is about deployment. And in order to

133

do that, you need a clear focus, a north star. And the best way to accomplish that is the purpose statement we've already discussed. This purpose articulation is not in the sense of a corporate-speak word salad mission statement—not something that's all "be the best at leveraging the synergies of whatever," but instead something that rings as authentic and clear about why you're in business.

It's about looking at everything through the lens of meaning that customers/members/audience has.

And we've talked about the need for data, to model the business and learn.

But there are some other principles that can help you navigate any transformative time, but especially digital transformation where there are so many options, where it can all get overwhelming.

Look for opportunities to use machine learning, AI, and automation to automate the tedious, repetitive tasks, but experiment with automating meaning into interactions, too, in the form of nuance, subtlety, and context.

Organizations want growth, but unqualified growth will pull you in all directions. What they need is *meaningful* growth. What meaningful growth requires is alignment: aligning the intentions of customers, the purpose of the organization, the talent of the employees, and the energy of the investors.

Keep One Eye on the Now and One Eye on the Future

I often talk about how meaningful growth requires keeping one eye on the now and one eye looking into the distant future.

My best story about this goes back to 2000 or 2001 or so, when I was at Netflix. At that point we were still ambitiously striving toward a million subscribers (they have a hundred million now), still very much the new kid on the block, and still engaged in all-out bloody war with Blockbuster.

Reed Hastings had the presence of mind to allocate budget and resources to R&D around streaming (although at the time we were talking about it in terms of "set-top boxes," which led the way to streaming). Again, this was in 2000. This was seven years before Roku launched, and seven years before Netflix had a streaming plan. DVDs were all anyone was really thinking about buying.

The traditional way to grow the business would have been to say, "We're a DVD rental company. Let's optimize our rental business and rent more stuff and look for ways to make more money by renting more stuff." But thinking about the opportunity from the standpoint of, "People pay us to be entertained in the comfort of their homes, so let's focus on getting them more entertainment to watch more easily," paid off in spades.

It has always stayed with me because that example of leadership was so visionary. So much about what has helped Netflix succeed has been the ability to see around corners. Reed Hastings and the rest of the company's leadership had the presence of mind to look ahead even while their own future was anything but certain.

And now the business Netflix is in today wouldn't have been possible without their early investments in direct streaming content. It freed them up to become content creators in their own right. No one in 2000 anticipated that Netflix's biggest competitors in 2017 would be Amazon, Disney, and sleep.

One eye on the now, so you know what's happening right in front of you, and one eye on the distant future, so you can align today's decisions with an understanding of evolving trends, the competitive landscape, and a vision of your purpose writ large.

Partner Up

It's helpful to think about business partnerships as akin to API thinking. Application Programming Interfaces are frameworks within software that build in "hooks" that can be extended and can integrate with other software and frameworks. Every company, every platform, every product could stand to think about what "hooks" they could potentially offer that could be integrated with other products for the convenience and experience of the end user or consumer, for a fuller offering.

The downside may be that no one owns the total experience, but it also broadens the reach of the brand and the experience so dramatically that it's a tradeoff worth considering.

Partnerships and business development offer this kind of thinking. Brands that recognize affinities their customers have with other noncompetitive brands may see opportunities to create an incentive for customers to sign up for both services or buy both products.

Certification programs are another way to accomplish this. I did some speaking and strategy consulting work with the Asthma and Allergy Foundation of America on their Allergy-Friendly certification program, in which companies like Dyson, Stanley Steemer, and others were participants. The benefits are significant across the brands of the holistic trust that comes from a consumer recognizing the certification icon on a package and transferring all of the trust they have in that certification to the product or service.

Make sure data is protected equally well.

Partnering could mean investing in up-and-coming entrants to the market, as well. For example, JetBlue Airways launched a venture company, JetBlue Technology Ventures, to invest in start-ups that combine an emphasis on travel, technology, and hospitality. Through their investment venture they can provide not only funding but also guidance to promising new companies, placing JetBlue in an ideal position to utilize solutions as they become market-ready and even acquire the companies if they're a fit. Similarly Dell has had a capital venture arm, Dell Technologies Capital, since 2012, with 148 investments that include 29 exits, including DocuSign and MongoDB which are both "unicorns" with valuations over $1Billion and are both now publicly traded[81].

Getting Ready to Evolve

What will come after this? After all, a strategy is not a roadmap, but it should be the step toward developing a roadmap and having greater clarity about what goes on it and in what order.

Your roadmap should include experience enhancement projects as well as cost savings projects.

What levers can you pull to get more revenue, and what are the costs and tradeoffs? In other words, where can you put resources that would result in incremental sales, whether those resources are advertising units or call center staff hours, etc.? And what kind of return will you get on that revenue, and does it align with your purpose objective?

CHAPTER 27

Evolve: Ready Your Business for the Future

WHAT DOES EVOLUTION LOOK LIKE in the context of emerging technologies? It takes changing mindsets as well as machines.

It was never a great approach to business to keep doing something the old way, but now if that's all you've got, it's lethal to the business. Resistance will only slow you down.

So how do you ready your business for the future, guard against platform disruption, and embrace emerging technology when it's relevant?

By looking objectively at the market, the opportunity, with a willingness to see the appeal in the future, to look at the opportunities from the perspective of both the good of the business and the good of humanity.

Disruption and Change

On one hand, I'm sentimental about bookstores, movie theaters, and radio. Many of my own meaningful experiences in life have involved settings and platforms that are fading into the past. On the other hand, I buy most of my new books electronically, I watch the majority of my movies online, and I listen to public radio programs via their podcasts. In fact, while I'm an avid fan of "radio," I don't own an actual radio. Still, there's something nostalgic about the fuzzy static sound I associate with scanning through the dial. And I don't want bookstores or movie theaters to go away, even though my consumer dollars are rarely spent with them.

I'm not unusual in this respect. Many people have emotional attachments to forms of experience they no longer support commercially. Streaming music channels have all but replaced the purchase of recorded albums, but plenty of people who grew up with record stores still feel nostalgic about them. The feel of newsprint and ink and the cumbersome size of the news sheet is, for many people, part and parcel of the news experience, even if they now get most of their updates from a publication's app, or from Twitter.

Of course within all these tradeoffs there are compelling experience features, which is why the old ways are falling aside in the first place. We can certainly mourn the potential loss of yellow cabs from New York City as a loss to the city's mythology and visual brand, but it's also tough to deny that the ubiquity of Uber and other rideshare vehicles, the convenience of hailing within the app, the predictability of pricing, and the ability to pay in an integrated way (note: there's our theme of integration again) are all features that have elevated people's expectations for their experience while getting from A to B.

Let's go back and look at the original disruption idea, introduced in 1995 in the *Harvard Business Review* (HBR)[82] by Clayton Christensen and subsequently expanded in his bestselling book, *The Innovator's Dilemma*. The idea suggests that a "disruptive" business enters a low-end market and moves it upstream to higher-value markets. Either that, or it creates a "new market foothold," which means it opens up a new market where there was none.[83]

For every disruption, there are enhancements most people widely agree are upgrades. From the packaging of seasons of TV shows on DVD in the 1990s through the on-demand streaming access provided by Netflix, Hulu, Amazon, and other online movie and TV services, we can now look back at "appointment television" as an anachronism most of us would probably not particularly wish to have back. Instead, though, the media-watching experience has changed so dramatically that we now talk in terms of binge-watching whole seasons of a show in a sitting. The work of crafting a narrative arc in the writing of a show has updated, but so have the business models that support the content development and distribution. Whereas advertisements during scheduled TV broadcasts were big business, the subscriptions paid to Netflix, for example, now fund more or less the entire content production lifecycle, with the consumer data available to the company to better understand not only what people are watching but subtle relationships between shows that people watch, which allows them to make and invest in more finely tuned programming.

Some old models seemed to work perfectly well. Some of them were even meaningful experiences in their day. Public radio, for example, which has long been supported partly by listener contributions and subscriptions, is one of the few industries I can think of that has its own term for meaningful experiences: "driveway moments," which describes a scenario where listeners have arrived home but sit in the car in the driveway not wanting to miss the end of the program. But a hefty portion of their listener base, and of their subscriber base—myself included—may not have driveways *or radios* at this point. As terrestrial radio becomes increasingly arcane and outdated, the industry has had to shift a substantial amount of programming and technical effort to podcasts and other formats.

Old beloved formats and platforms may lose out to new, disruptive platforms if they don't keep up with technology trends and cultural expectations. It's inevitable if we don't understand the necessity for change. It's true for public radio, bookstores, movie theaters, retail, magazines, TV channels, and more. How can these media and platforms adapt to the opportunities of digitization without losing their integrity?

Once again, we need to start from purpose, and embrace thinking about the future as discussed in Keep One Eye on the Now and One Eye on the Future. The best way to navigate the changes emerging technology will bring about is to focus on making human experiences more meaningful; we just have to do so with an eyes-wide-open awareness of the context of changing cultural expectations all around us.

Renewal, Recurrence, and Loyalty Models

In a utopian Tech Humanist world, no one has to worry about running out of a product they depend on because thanks to ubiquitous or context-appropriate interfaces, as well as logistics that lead to quick delivery, it's always simple to get more just when you need it. But also —and this is just as important—no one has to worry about being pestered to renew something they don't want anymore.

To get there, businesses must figure out how often people will *truly* want to use your product and either what makes its reuse compelling or what the appropriate subsequent product in a sequence is.

If I've bought an expensive appliance, like a washing machine, I obviously won't want to repurchase that same expensive appliance again, but I may very much appreciate the opportunity to buy timely refills of supplies for the appliance, such as laundry detergent, and in some cases I may like the option to subscribe to content that helps me continue to feel excited about my purchase. When I finally made the decision to buy a Vitamix blender some years ago after years of coveting them, the retailer missed out on an opportunity I would have welcomed to make occasional outreach via email or social media or wherever I'd given them permission about recipes and usage tips and so on.

Some products also come with great opportunities to build community around the product with other purchasers of the product.

In any case, you have to get *both* the experience model right *and* the data model and technology deployment right.

If you offer a product or service that people will want regularly, optimize for ease of recurring revenue. The more you can make the experience seamless and compelling, the more it's a win-win.

This is true for subscription models of any sort, whether content subscriptions like news and magazines or product subscriptions like Amazon Subscribe and Save, Harry's Razors, or my cats' favorite pet food auto-ship feature on <u>Chewy.com</u>.

Another model that may be worth exploring is subscription boxes, which combine monthly or periodic recurring revenue with curated goods. Blue Apron is a great example of a food prep service, and there are who-knows-how-many clothing subscription boxes. It takes plenty of backend technology to make this viable and scalable, and you need an ecosystem of providers and suppliers. But if the model and the experience are aligned, what a powerful way to create a trusted relationship with people who look forward to the shipments every month.

A whole raft of tech-enabled options are emerging to make these processes even simpler, such as the Amazon Dash button, and other Internet of Things integrations for on-demand refills of household items.

How can you make all this meaningful for customers, while deepening the relationship between them and your brand?

CHAPTER 28

Ethics at Scale

AN ENTIRE ECOSYSTEM OF CHANGES is happening around human existence, responding to and altering human potential with every movement, decision, and interaction. The decisions that develop the systems creating these changes are responsible for the experiences that scale into behaviors, into language, into culture, into social norms, and into the fabric of our future. As we integrate more data, more digital responsiveness, more agility into our businesses, we need to consider carefully what impact the decisions and strategies will have on human experience at large.

The ethical implications alone of the combined set of big data, algorithms, automation, and artificial intelligence have justifiably already been the subject of many books and will undoubtedly be explored in many to come. Because the Tech Humanist approach inherently recognizes business drivers as the dominant accelerating force behind the rise of emerging technologies, my focus in this chapter is primarily on issues found at the intersection of the following two considerations:

- What are the ethical considerations of and risks associated with the broadening use of human data in business digital transformation?

- What are the threats to human liberty and justice in a future that relies on machines to create human experiences?

The latter question alone, though, is a sprawling and profound topic and deserves inquiry by anyone concerned about the human impacts of automation and algorithmic experiences. If you want to explore the intricacies of the impact to human social justice from automation and artificial intelligence more fully beyond the context of how business applications cause technologies to scale, I can highly recommend adding the following books to your queue for further reading:

- *Weapons of Math Destruction: How Big Data Increases Inequality and Threatens Democracy* by Cathy O'Neil
- *Automating Inequality: How High-Tech Tools Profile, Police, and Punish the Poor* by Virginia Eubanks
- *Technically Wrong: Sexist Apps, Biased Algorithms, and Other Threats of Toxic Tech* by Sara Wachter-Boettcher

Additionally, organizations like Data & Society[84] and the AI Now Institute[85], both of which I admire greatly, are contributing in an ongoing way to the knowledge and standards in these fields. Their websites are provided in the footnotes.

At a more fundamental level, many of the philosophical questions we have long posed as mere thought experiments are becoming vividly real with unprecedented potential impact. The old "trolley problem" that poses a dilemma about the risk of multiple lives versus one has deepened meaning and scale when applied to the algorithmic encoding of autonomous vehicles, and what those decisions could mean for society.[86]

If AI can detect medical problems like cancer more reliably than human doctors and radiologists, then isn't the ethical thing to do to use AI and treat the patient? What precautions do we need to take to ensure the algorithms behind the AI aren't racially biased, or that they aren't optimizing for cost savings rather than patient health?[87]

Even what seem like a useful idea can have unintended consequences and potentially nefarious side effects.

In 2017, iRobot, the makers of the popular Roomba automated

vacuum cleaner, revealed plans to sell mapped layouts of customers' homes. The intent was to further the effectiveness of the other smart home automation devices on the market, since most of them were still pretty, well, dumb about the whereabouts of anything within the house. In theory, that sharing of data could make the whole home automation promise more of a reality. Meanwhile, the Roomba was becoming smarter about the layout of the house in ways that could further its own sophistication and capability, potentially making it possible, for example, for it to respond to instructions to clean a particular room. But it also raises legitimate privacy concerns about the safety of customers' home data and whose hands that data lands in.

In many boardrooms, though—*too* many boardrooms—any discussion of ethics can seem abstract and high-minded. I generally avoid the term "business ethics" since it seems to imply that there is some kind of business exception to "normal" ethics, but the Tech Humanist mindset realizes that it's all integrated: The scale of human impacts from technology is growing, and that business is the primary driver of that growth. We know that algorithms, big data, AI, and automation force consideration of ethics at scale. That said, business leaders will do well to remember that along with the human responsibility that comes with hiring people and serving the public, there are quantifiable risks to the bottom line from all this, too, from legal compliance with emerging regulations such as the European Union's General Data Protection Regulation (GDPR)[88], and if you're not considering it carefully enough, your employees and shareholders just might remind you.

After Amazon introduced real-time facial recognition services in late 2016, they began selling those services to law enforcement and government agencies, such as the Orlando Police Department and Washington County, Oregon[89]. But the technology raises major privacy concerns; the police could use the technology not only to track people who are suspected of having committed crimes, but also people who are *not* committing crimes, such as protestors and others whom the police deem a nuisance. It's probably not surprising to note that the American Civil Liberties Union (ACLU) asked Amazon to stop selling this service, but it may surprise you to hear that a portion of both Amazon's shareholders and employees asked Amazon to stop, as well, citing concerns for the company's valuation and reputation given the risk of misapplication and public outcry.

The fullness of how technology stands to impact humanity is tough to overstate. The opportunity exists for us to make it better, but to do that, we also have to recognize some of the ways in which it can get worse. Once we understand the issues, it's up to all of us to weigh in on how we want to see the future play out.

Tremendous Potential for Change…And Even Greater Inequality

The potential of automation and artificial intelligence is unlike any economic factor the world has yet known, and their implementation could generate unprecedented economic growth. But inherently something with this much power also runs great risk, and those risks carry outsized consequences. The World Economic Forum has cautioned that AI could potentially make financial markets more vulnerable[90], increasing the risk of cyberattacks, and concentrating wealth and power even more greatly, leading to even greater inequality.

We have an opportunity to develop logistical, moral, ethical, financial, and other incentives for ensuring that humans have more equal opportunities and resources.

Social tools have amplified human potential and reach to the point of effecting major social change, such as with the Arab Spring uprising in Egypt, the 2013 citizen uprising that led to the ouster of Tunisian president Zine El Abidine Ben Ali, and the overthrow of Egyptian President Hosni Mubarak that was helped along by the digital connectedness of protestors being able to communicate and organize at scale in real-time.

Inevitably, various technologies have already begun to reveal bias against groups of individuals with historic and systemic disadvantages, which furthers the already rampant systemic inequality and makes conditions even tougher for the poor and marginalized. Amplified by algorithms, facial recognition and other policing technologies disproportionately amplify the policing of the poor, and a trust in these technologies reflects itself in the criminal justice system.

We have to anticipate potentially limiting impacts on employment, insurance, and housing options.

Some of the differences take shape from past purchases and browsing history, and lead to other data leading to limited offers available, different prices available, and so on.

And of course we can't forget the economic and social implications of human job displacement and replacement due to automation and AI.

But with a both/and mindset, we can see that the reverse side is also true: Human potential is everywhere, and solutions that treat individuals with respect while looking for the best outcomes for everyone are the ones most likely to do the most good and be the most sustainably successful. Look at prisoner education programs. Compared to the $30,000 per year it costs to incarcerate someone, it only costs $5,000 per year to provide a former inmate with training and skills—job skills and soft skills that help them adapt to life beyond prison—to succeed and make a dignified contribution to society. And some programs, like EDWINS Leadership & Restaurant Institute in Cleveland, are thorough enough and executed well enough that their recidivism rates are near zero.

If we want the best futures for the most people, we have to seize the opportunity to use technology to represent a range of humanity. Use diversity and inclusion in telling the stories of humanity and developing the technologies that serve humanity. Train algorithms and machine learning with data sets that represent as diverse a human population as possible.

Looking for Ethics in Silicon Valley and Beyond

Much of what is flawed about society in the twenty-first century is that we *have* in many ways maximized the worst of human impulses, creating a spiraling race to the bottom of humanity's worst instincts. How can we monetize greed? How can we monetize shame? How can we monetize addictive behaviors?

But at least we did so with older, slower technology.

If we allow the accelerated technologies of today and tomorrow to amplify these questionable motives and instincts, we are in for a future we don't want to imagine. And we have to collectively agree to be part of a better version of the future; we can't "get ours" and leave others to do better work.

Ethics and far-reaching considerations must now be part of every strategic decision, because the consequences of making the wrong things scale are too steep.

Consider, for example, the problems that have plagued Twitter during its rise as a social platform in the late 2000s and 2010s. The issues that surfaced at the height of Gamergate—that certain users were acting in bad faith, were threatening physical violence, etc.— outlined the shape of the issues. There were issues of access privileges, free speech, hate speech, and public safety wrapped up in the mix. Twitter's overall leadership and those responsible for setting and enacting policy relative to banning users had the opportunity to philosophize or take action. During 2018's confrontation with white supremacists and particularly the issue of whether or not to ban Alex Jones and InfoWars from the platform, their actions have been slow. With the scale that comes from technology also comes the responsibility to determine safety, access, and rights for vast numbers of participants across geographic jurisdictions.

It's perhaps not an easy thing to find yourself leading a company that unexpectedly sits squarely at the heart of the issues of free speech in a connected era. In interviews, Jack Dorsey, the CEO of Twitter, has adopted an outwardly philosophical approach, seemingly giving weight to a sense of fairness toward each user's right to express anything short of violent harm, rather than giving weight to what affects the good of the most users.

What are the legal and ethical obligations of a platform in balancing free speech versus safety to its users? How does that change with scale?

In Jack Dorsey's September 2018 testimony before Congress, he talked about Twitter as a "public square"; and that metaphor, that framework is actually one of the keys to the debate about the effective management of that space. Because it is a corporately owned entity, it is more of a parallel to instances of public-private spaces in many cities, like New York, that involve both corporate ownership and public access rights. Which one wins out depends on how you choose to center that discussion, and given the scale of the consequences, I'm in favor of centering human experiences, human safety, and the good of humanity as a whole, while working to make corporate incentives align and scale with the best outcomes for humans. It's much harder to retrofit meaningful human outcomes around profit-driven objectives than the other way around.

> It's much harder to retrofit meaningful human outcomes around profit-driven objectives than the other way around.

To what extent is the underlying business model responsible for influencing the leadership's decision? Since the Tech Humanist approach is about purpose and alignment, it might seem as if the decisions that align with an advertising-based business model would inherently be best. But an advertising platform is itself an inherently misaligned business platform, and to make it human-centric requires deliberate efforts to align with a purpose greater than advertising.

For example, the Google AdWords advertising platform has always benefited most from relevance and alignment with the user's mission of finding answers to a search query. While an entire industry of search engine optimization grew around the enhancement (and sometimes manipulation) of web content to suit the organic (nonpaid) results on Google, a parallel discipline also emerged around maximizing return on ad spend within paid search results in AdWords. The ranking factors have always been conceptually similar: The best results shared clarity of messaging, alignment between query and content, well-structured pages, and an absence of certain manipulative tricks to game the system. Advanced techniques differ between the organic and paid platforms, but at a fundamental level, the searcher's intent was to find the most relevant information compared with other methods of discovery; Google's intent was to offer the most relevant results compared with other methods of discovery; and the content creator's intent was to get in front of people who are searching for the very thing they offer and to make it the most relevant and compelling compared with other offers. Relevance was the value that aligned all of the participants in the model. So while one could expect challenges to emerge here and there in that model as it scales, it stands a pretty good chance of scaling with all participants' experience in proportion to one another. Moreover, all the actors who participate in good faith can expect reasonably good outcomes. The actors who participate in bad faith can expect eventual bad outcomes.

An advertising-based social platform is more challenging to align. The inherent value proposition of the platform is more ambiguous, such as on Facebook: Is it "to keep up with friends"? If so, in that metaphor, advertisers who show up in the feed are friends by proxy, an embellishment which may please the advertiser but isn't a truthful experience for the vast majority of human end users.

That may be part of the explanation for the outsized role content on Facebook plays in influencing public opinion. The metaphorical origins of the service have conditioned users at some level to think of what we read in our feed as "keeping up with friends," but as Facebook itself demonstrated with its covert and widely criticized psychological experiment, the experience maximizes human impulses and leads to a changed emotional state, for better or worse. Combine this with the extreme filter bubble effects of increased algorithmic optimization and the polarization of content exposure, and you have a powder keg situation.

From a business leadership standpoint, you can always think about it in terms of risk reduction. While you might enjoy having Mark Zuckerberg's resources and power, you probably wouldn't want to sit where Mark Zuckerberg sits when he's testifying in front of Congress and facing penalties for failing to act in a transparent way with data that shapes the experiences of those who use his company's service.

Are there business models we should inherently question? Is advertising as a mechanism to support a free service that operates on the aggregation and exploitation of people's shared data inherently faulty or not humanist?

Of course there's the old adage that if you're not paying, you are the product.

Platforms such as Facebook, Twitter, LinkedIn, and Google are also able to function as authentication for other services, so there's an overlay in digital experience (which increasingly intersects with physical experience) that can be targeted through social graph, work history, email history, personal data, and so much more. This has always offered mind-boggling potential for personalized, tailored, ultrarelevant experiences and content, while it also increases risk of identity theft, unethical targeting, algorithmic manipulation, gamified data harvesting, and other kinds of hacking.

The Cambridge Analytica issue demonstrates how many data points connected with accounts that were exploited, and the influence they have had on not only the 2016 US presidential election but also on political dynamics worldwide is still being sorted out.

Again, all of this becomes of paramount importance with the continued increase of and reliance on algorithmic optimization of news content and other media, and the automation of experiences in, around, and connected to these platforms.

One of the clear implications of the accelerating platforms is a need for greater media literacy, information ethics, and informed citizenry.

So how do we champion a Tech Humanist future in the face of that? What should we be asking ourselves to do? What should we be holding ourselves accountable for?

Realistically we may not be able to incentivize private business away from whatever makes them money. But as humans and consumers, we can be willing to lobby with our wallets and our data. As business leaders, we can make ethical choices about aligning the objectives of our businesses and the people we serve. And as citizens and voters, we can demand a government that provides the appropriate regulation to protect humans—who, because these are evolving platforms and systems so sophisticated experts have trouble keeping up, don't always know the fullness of what's at stake.

Ethical Obligations of Experience Creators

In *Pixels and Place*, I wrote about the metaphors of space. But I never overtly said—and it is clearer to me now—that when someone creates a space, whether physical or digital, they are also assuming some degree of responsibility for what happens there, and what happens to people who come to use that space in sanctioned ways. And even unsanctioned ways, in some cases.

So what are the ethical obligations of experience creators? To offer space to connect, liberate, and communicate when developing an interaction, a community, a platform, or even a hashtag conversation?

But then what are the ethical obligations of experience creators to offer safety and "shelter," maintain it, and offer protections to the people who participate in the experience?

A memo written by Facebook vice president Andrew Bosworth while he was overseeing the advertising and business platform included some moral equivocating about whether the company was producing value even if someone died in connection with services provided by the platform.

"Maybe it costs a life by exposing someone to bullies," he wrote in the memo, according to BuzzFeed News. "Maybe someone dies in a terrorist attack coordinated on our tools. And still we connect people. The ugly truth is that we believe in connecting people so deeply that anything that allows us to connect more people more often is *de facto* good."

After BuzzFeed published its report, Bosworth later tweeted: "I didn't agree with it even when I wrote it." He is now in charge of the company's virtual reality department.

Virtual reality itself brings up two-fold questions of responsibility and ethical obligations in terms of the safety and well-being of users of the technology: 1) How safe and well-considered are the virtual environments the creators design, and can they cause harm visually, psychologically, or emotionally? 2) How safe are the physical spaces where users immerse themselves in the experience? The former is well within the experience creator's scope, at least for genuine consideration if not out-and-out responsibility. The latter would seem to fall more under the realm of educating users about safe and appropriate use, and like so many matters of technological literacy, that responsibility is often avoided by experience creators.

An inherent problem lies in the abstract "thought experiment" mentality of so many people working in tech leadership roles. They are themselves often abstracted from the dangers and realities of the risks that are amplified by tools like social platforms that connect terrorists, bullies, racists, and so on. To them it's all just an interesting question to ponder, with very little real life consequence.

A source I recommend for further reading on this is *Design for Real Life* by Eric Meyer and Sara Wachter-Boettcher, which explores designing for stress cases beyond idealized use cases and designing interfaces and experiences with compassion for the real life scenarios people often bring to them.

Broadly speaking, companies investing in emerging technologies for human use such as VR, AI, and wearables and the people developing them need to consult with sociologists, linguists, ethicists, and other social scientists to better understand the wider implications and ramifications of their decisions.

Algorithmic, AI, and Automation Transparency and Disclosure

It seems like an easy position to take that humans deserve to know when we're dealing with machines and artificial intelligence, when algorithms are determining the outcome of our interactions, and so on —basically whenever we're at risk of being manipulated by data models with predictive capabilities that can coax us to spend more, or agree to things that may not be in our best interest. But in practice the models are often interwoven into hybrid operations that involve human oversight and interactions. It's not always clear when a machine is making decisions in a transaction and when a human is doing so. So there are big questions about when and how machine-led interactions should reveal that they are machines. See Should a Bot Have to Tell You It's a Bot for more on this.

If you're developing any kind of AI program for your organization, consider how and when you will disclose to people. But the matter of what transparency in AI looks like and means in practice is still being resolved. Our decisions in using AI in human-facing applications now will set important precedents for what happens as the capabilities of AI grow and along with them, the scope of AI deployments.

But when it comes to how and when to disclose when algorithms or AI are involved in decision-making, it gets a little murky. Again, in most business environments, AI isn't an all-or-nothing replacement for humans; in some of the best use cases, AI augments human intelligence and decision-making rather than replacing it. In addition, while an overlay, popup indicator, or other visual cue might be effective (if also potentially annoying) in a screen-based interaction, we also need standards for non-screen interactions and functions, such as those that happen through the Internet of Things. More and more we need to assume machines are part of the process, so the ethical and logistical standards still need to be developed for user interface mechanisms, and regulations on their consistent use, that indicate when and why algorithms and AI are involved, how they're involved, what factors they consider, what sources of data they may be looking at, and so on.

No matter what, we must work to reduce bias and encode the highest of human values.

Truth and Trust in a Algorithmically-Optimized World

I can almost hear the voice-over to the movie trailer of our times: "IN A WORLD...WHERE SOULLESS ALGORITHMS DETERMINE THE STORIES YOU CAN SEE, AND THE TRUTH YOU ARE ALLOWED TO KNOW..."

How do we know when we are being presented with the truth? How can we trust the sources?

By now, the "filter bubble" phenomenon is well-known to most people. Eli Pariser wrote and spoke about the self-perpetuating effects of recommendation algorithms in 2011, and we've since seen the effects of bots and automation on human society in various ways — one notorious example being the 2016 US presidential election.

But the version of the filter bubble that Eli Pariser was speaking and writing about in 2011 is nothing compared with the hyper-filtered reality bubble digital citizens dwell within seven years later, thanks to years of affinity and recommendation algorithms, bots and automated scripts arbitrarily amplifying reactive behavior on shared content, and predictive algorithms and machine learning set up to try to optimize people's reading and buying habits for advertising and other profit motives. And that's simply going to happen more and more.

It will take active efforts to correct our course.

Can we trust the data? The machines? The algorithms?

Well, if we have followed the Tech Humanist approach and encoded them with the best of ourselves, we should be at least better able to trust them.

But is truth a human ideal? Is it something to strive for? Are there always relative truths?

After all, this kind of nuance and philosophical relativism is not necessarily AI's strong suit, and algorithms only work with what they're given.

The bigger question is: Can we trust *ourselves* in the data, machine, and algorithms?

Can we trust the humans who encoded the machines? How do we know their values? How do we know their motives?

We come back to the mechanics of meaning and nuance. If we have no capacity for understanding a worldview that is not based on polar ends of a spectrum, we will repeatedly fail.

How can we hope to have alignment if common end points are not understood, and how can common end points be understood if truth is relative?

In practice, those questions break down into:

How much can we trust the *sources* of news and other content?

- How can we ascertain the veracity of news media, and "fake news"?
- How do we know the biases and perspectives of media and online content?
- How do we deal with the growing effects of the "filter bubble"?
- Should we limit ourselves to what is algorithmically recommended?

But also, **how much can we trust the content itself?**

For some years now we've had a cultural awareness about the feasibility of image manipulation with Photoshop and other powerful image editing tools, but videos have seemed more credible because we sense they're harder to fake. But with AI technologies to synthesize images and videos, visual proof that appears real will be easily faked—a phenomenon already appearing as videos with facial images replaced or voices altered known as "deepfakes"[91] (a portmanteau of "deep learning" and "fake"). These are becoming trivial to make. Some will be easily detected, too, using the same or equivalent technologies. But some will escape machine detection, and humans will be left to assess and respond.

There are legitimate and interesting commercial uses for these technologies, such as altering the facial expressions of actors in movies when the audio is dubbed over with translated dialogue[92]. But many of the uses will be for subversion, discord, counterculture, and pranks. And they will sow chaos.

How can we recognize faked content, like pictures and video?

In a similar vein, we will see increases in adversarial attacks on machine learning systems—in other words, inputs designed to trick a system's processing limitations. While there are arguably defensible uses in terms of thwarting overzealous application of AI tools, such as a grassroots use of masks that foil facial recognition by law enforcement using facial recognition to scan the crowds at peaceful public demonstrations, most of the "legitimate" and "illegitimate" use cases of any technology are bound to be somewhat in the eye of the beholder.

Take, for example, the artist James Bridle, whose viral video showed that pouring salt around an autonomous vehicle in a solid circle with dashes outside of it "trapped" it since road logic says you can't cross a solid line with dashes on the other side.[93]

How can we design and develop experiences for people at scale with a full awareness of these challenges, taking full advantage of the tools when it makes sense to do so, and dealing with them ethically?

How might AI help us sort out truth rather than obfuscate it?

How do we cross this gap, resolve this dilemma?

Furthermore, how much can we trust our surroundings?

Think about the VR space. Using goggles and other equipment to obstruct ambient sensory data so you can augment them with virtual input relies on a trusted environment and a code of conduct with other players and surrounding people. Even Pokémon GO! and other games, apps, and tools that don't require complete obstruction often induce people to partial obstruction by looking down at screens or holding screens up in front of their faces.

Another consideration for how to improve human experience is how to remove these impediments when they're not meaningful to the experience—and when the impediments to sensory input *are* meaningful, to consider how to make them feel safe and be part of a trustworthy environment.

Once again it comes back to respect for human life and human dignity as a value. If we can trust that that respect is there, encoded into the data, built into the surroundings, we can lean into the progress that comes with technological advances.

Already, our society is desperately in need of cultivating more media literacy, digital literacy, and technology literacy. People need an evolved kind of media literacy: separating fact from opinion, separating credible truth from propaganda, reading motive into media, questioning bias, etc.

That need only grows with the increase of algorithmically optimized and AI-created content. We need to help people better understand how they can interpret the credibility of the content they consume, the sources they consume it from, the experiences they have, and the surroundings they're in.

Because in trying to achieve meaningful, relevant, contextual communication and experiences, we must recognize that the perspectives of the participants matter. There will continue to be a need for storytelling, for conveying the essence of an idea. In other words, if you're trying to have a meaningful conversation with someone, the more you understand of their motives, their background knowledge, and the context your conversation is taking place within, the more understanding you can share.

Human Imitation by Machines

Why does it break our hearts when R2D2 makes sad sounds? Why do the challenges WALL-E faces tug at our heartstrings? What is happening to make these fictional robots humanlike enough or worthy of our compassion and empathy?

One part of the explanation is that researchers have found neurological links in the compassion we instinctively feel for robots and for humans[94]. The same kind of reactions occur in the brain when we observe robots and humans in pain, although multiple studies suggest we do tend to feel more empathy for humans, and our empathy reactions for humanoid robots is a little slower as it takes us a bit longer to put ourselves in the robot's place.

But without question, robot designers are intentionally using human empathy to create bonds with robots, including humanlike physique, facial expressions, and interactions.

Children's toys from just a few years ago were designed with static expressions meant to be pleasing and bonding, but the toys being designed now may include animated expressions to create a deeper bond with children.[95] As positive as this experience might be for children, the idea causes concern that children may transfer that bond to other technology, even surfacing concern over "virtual enslavement[96]." It's not a misguided concern: In fact, toys have been used as lures for children into kidnapping or trafficking schemes, so it is not inconceivable that toys mimicking human expressions can be horribly misused.

We must keep our eyes wide open to the possible problems. But first we need to come to a more integrated place with technology.

After all, robots will be a significant factor in the home health care industry, as helpers to humans in hospital and elder care settings.

Add to that the rise of a whole category of voice-based AI assistants increasingly being designed to sound human. With voice interactions becoming increasingly common and virtual assistants gaining ground, one obvious opportunity was to combine a virtual assistant with a voice that sounds human. Google Duplex voice assistant, as one of the most visible examples, can make calls on a person's behalf—such as to make restaurant reservations—and it includes pauses and speech irregularities[97] to sound more convincingly human. What are the longer-term ethical implications of this? Like any impersonation of humans by machine, like any Tech Humanist implementation, it comes down to how aligned the objectives are. Deceiving one human to accomplish the objectives of another leaves us on shaky ethical ground.

Can we add this kind of interaction in a way that isn't about manipulating or deceiving humans but instead is about aligning business and human objectives, aligning human objectives with each other, and accelerating toward an aligned outcome?

So if you're writing copy for robotic interactions, whether they take place via text or voice, the best approach is to aim for a brand-aligned voice and tone, be brief and to the point, and work to achieve the aligned goals of the interaction, not deception of the human using the service.

Whether it's smartphones or voice assistants, we need to seek the right balance of connectedness with technology and a healthy balance of time and emotional investment, as well as a healthy skepticism about the motives it's being used to advance.

How can we elevate all of these efforts from the gee-whiz cool factor of creating human-ish or humanlike interactions to focusing on making a more human-centric one, ensuring that as Tech Humanists we are creating more meaningful experiences?

The point of designing human-centric technology is not to make technology more human, per se; the point is to make any tech align with business goals *and* with human goals. Sometimes that means making it feel humanlike or human-ish, and sometimes we're all better off if the robot remains robotlike. But either way, the key is to dimensionalize the business goals into a strategy for technology deployment and data collection that can make the organization smarter, more responsive, and better able to provide meaningful experiences.

Should a Bot Have to Tell You It's a Bot

Let's say you have a question about your bank account, so you visit your bank's website to find a phone number to call them. While you're looking for that, a chat box pops up in the corner of the window, prompting you to chat live with an agent for help. *Why not?* you think, and start to type.

So far so good. But let's say your question is about how to protect your account from your ex-spouse or ex-partner who may still have access. As you begin to explain the situation, the chat agent asks you questions about your account, and eventually recommends that you create a new, separate account into which you can move your money.

At any point, are you concerned that the agent has fully understood your situation before making this recommendation? Would your comfort level change if you knew that the agent was in fact a rules-based, machine-driven chatbot?

Let's pause to define our terms. For the purposes of this discussion, a bot is the conversational interface for a product or a brand or other entity that uses programmed logic and in some cases machine learning to determine how to interact around a specified topic or function — such as placing an order, initiating a customer support request, etc.

You're interacting with a machine in what feels like a very conversational way.

So in the example above, should the bank have disclosed that you were chatting with a bot? Should it be required to? If so, at what point? From the beginning, or only once your interaction reached a certain level of sophistication?

In other words, would it be okay if the extent of your interactions with the bot were about logging in to the website and retrieving a forgotten password?

Various banks have tried this. The ability to automate the interaction about one of the most frequent and simplest customer support issues has shown some banks considerable potential for return. And customers don't seem too bothered about it; after all, it's not that different from clicking a "forgot password" link and having a system email a password reset link to you.

Consumers Want Results

In a 2016 study from Aspect, a company that works in customer service optimization, over 70 percent of consumers surveyed said they wanted the ability to solve most customer service issues on their own. Almost half said they'd prefer to conduct all customer service interactions via text, chat, or messaging "if the company could get it right." And most indicated they already interact with an intelligent assistant or chatbot at least once per month.[98]

In fact, several experiments from Goldsmiths University and global media agency Mindshare concluded that most consumer attitudes seem to fall somewhere between "would consider" to "would prefer" communicating with a chatbot while interacting with a business or brand.[99]

But there's a catch: As many as half said it would feel "creepy" if a bot pretended to be human.

Even at this early stage, there's an expectation that if you interact with a brand's bot, you're dealing with a machine that should feel like a machine. If you're offered fixed options and limited syntax, most people with any familiarity with bots would assume that they're interacting with a machine and would be surprised if they learned a human was involved at all.

The implication seems to be that consumers prefer whatever takes care of their issue, but they don't want to feel deceived in the process, and the distinction should be clear.

For perspective, I asked Ian Barkin, who is Co-Founder and Chief Strategy Officer at Symphony Ventures, as well as a member of the IEEE Working Group on Intelligent Process Automation. "My PoV has always been that bots enable 'people to do their best work.' So, there should be no shame in divulging when/where a bot is doing the routine so that, when you need the real hand-holding and support, there are good people who can spend the right amount of time supporting you."

But part of the challenge in making the transition to a more machine-scaled economy is that in our cultural conversation about automated interactions, we have such a divided understanding of human versus machine roles. In reality, as Ian says, a lot of customer support and technical support environments are not exclusively one or the other but rather human *plus* automation, where the most frequently asked questions or the questions with the simplest answers are where the automation scripts begin, and then humans can fill in around the edge cases.

This leaves the waters a bit murky when it comes to considering where and when a bot should have to disclose that it's a bot. The standards don't exactly exist for how to communicate that, or what the company should say about the data of yours it's using to create its side of the interactions.

For clarity, perhaps it's worth pondering why we want or need to know that a bot is a bot. The implication is that there's risk, so what is it that is at risk?

But Humans Are Hesitant to Go All In

Almost everyone I asked was initially bullish on bots for the sake of efficient customer service interactions, but they began to express reservations when they thought about interacting with a bot without knowing it was a bot.

None of us exist as consumers all the time. It's a role we inhabit from moment to moment, like parent, student, user, visitor, and so on. We're humans first and foremost, and our interactions with our fellow humans are sophisticated, nuanced, emotionally intelligent, and rich. So part of what we seem to envision when interacting with a human service agent is a match of human wit against human wit—a "fair fight." Intuitively, we may feel we can use all of our instinct, guile, and cunning to persuade a human to resolve an issue in our favor, or to resist a human's efforts to upsell or persuade us toward a particular outcome. We can use deductive reasoning and emotional intelligence and all of the other tools we may have within us to be able to deal with that. But pitted against a machine with—at least theoretically—access to vast arrays of data from which to draw patterns, with unyielding algorithmic logic, and potentially neural network learning systems, it seems like an unwinnable argument.

After all, if now a machine can beat human at Go and at chess, what chance do we have to resist a bot's offer to open a store account for an extra 10 percent off?

To be clear, though, at the moment, most chatbots aren't AI, at least not in any imagined sophisticated sense. The majority use a pretty straightforward form of rules-based processing—which means that in a support setting, they're fundamentally following the same rules a human agent would have to follow. So in terms of how a transaction is executed, it may make little difference whether a bot or a human is conducting the interaction.

But still to most of the people I surveyed, it feels like we deserve to know *somehow* when we're dealing with a machine that is mimicking human interactions. And further, that we should somehow be able to find out what factors involving our data the algorithms working behind the scenes are considering in processing our interactions.

We will get to a point where we have standards for how to communicate about this and what to expect, but some of our hesitation may be that we don't have a lot of practice yet at interacting with machines in situations where we typically rely on humans and where there's ambiguity in the interaction.

After all, most of the automation that's been introduced into our interactions over the years has been pretty overt. We know we're at an ATM and not dealing with a human teller, for example. Before some machines began dispensing different bill denominations, no amount of sweet-talking would convince the ATM to give you five-dollar bills; it was built to give you twenties, and that was that.

The scenario is no longer that clear-cut, and the machine interactions of the future may be even more ambiguous. Who has the power to make overriding decisions and when?

Reality Is Complicated

In developing chat-driven interactive systems, there is sometimes a transitional stage where interactions are scripted but humans drive the "back end" of the interactions. This always reminds me of Moviefone Kramer: the episode of *Seinfeld* where Kramer gets a new phone number and it's only one digit off from Moviefone, the pre-internet era automated phone service that you could call to determine movie showtimes. When George calls Kramer thinking he's called Moviefone and Kramer can't decipher George's touchtone entries, he amends the instructions: "Why don't you just tell me what movie you'd like to see?"

This is the sort of inverse uncanny valley of automated interaction: where a human interacts with a system expecting a machine and gets a human instead. So there's not always a very clear-cut distinction between when you're interacting with a human and when an automated process has intervened.

There's also a tremendous range of applications with different considerations and different needs for sensitivity and a sense of human respect. Retail, for example, may be one of the more obvious and in some ways least consequential applications of conversational bots. But when you really think about the many contexts in which a bot could be interacting with a human, they're nearly endless: financial services, healthcare, traveler support, entertainment, public safety, education, or even therapy. So if these interactions all potentially need some kind of disclosure that they are bot-based, the line would be pretty blurry about when it needs to be disclosed and when it doesn't.

Each of these contexts may have varying practical considerations that would determine whether disclosure is important. So before any kind of regulations might be proposed, a pretty thorough assessment would need to be made of the breadth of opportunities and how they might impact humans.

In the meantime, we can assume that more and more of our interactions are going to be augmented by automation and by machine learning in some way. What's important for companies developing their intelligent assistant programs, beyond disclosure, is to design with the human need in mind. For example, they should ensure that the transition from bot to human is seamless: 88 percent of customers said they expect a live agent who steps in after a bot begins the interaction to have all of the context—name, account number, etc.—that the customer has already provided.[100] That's about efficiency, but it's also about respect and human consideration, and no matter what, we can always use more of that.

Encode Technology with the Best of Humanity

It's not just that we need to try not to be overtly biased in the development of algorithms and the processing of data, although that would be a start.

But let's actually try to think ahead of the norms and dictates of the present moment and develop business rules and logic that look to our most enlightened selves. Can the data model be more inclusive? Can the algorithm acknowledge more diversity? Can the predictive algorithms we develop for law enforcement, healthcare, insurance, and beyond look deeper than the most obvious, surface characteristics of people's data and not deepen systemic divides?

CHAPTER 29

Design for Meaning

WHEN THE "RUBBER" OF MEANING and purpose meets the "road" of experience design, we need to know how to put the abstract into more concrete terms. What are the tools and frameworks of using data/tech/automation/AI to design meaningful human experiences? How can we really *design* meaningful human experiences?

Let's be clear on what we mean by meaningful experiences. As stated in Why Human Experience Matters, "meaningful experiences are those that have depth and memorability, that are significant because of how they transcend their context or complement their context."

How we achieve that is through empathy, context awareness, and an understanding of how the experience will come across in an integrated way. This next section explains Integrated Human Experience Design, a framework I introduced in *Pixels and Place*, and introduces the concept of applying this approach to automated environments.

Part of the approach is in understanding nature and shape (Consider Both Nature and Shape of Experiences), so we'll dig into that.

All of this will establish a baseline, too, for how to design experiences for humans that can be administered by machines and taken to scale without fear of amplifying bias, absurdity, or other malign conditions in the world around us.

This chapter includes some principles to address all of these considerations.

Integrated Human Experience Design

When we talk about experiences, we're talking about touchpoints, brand encounters, interactions, transactions, triggers, WoM discussions, in-store visits, etc.—a wide range of multidimensional possibilities.

Which means: We have to think about the data model, the technology deployment, the call center processes, the overall cultural alignment.

Even when we develop journey maps for people, they tend to be along an idealized sequence of events, and we leave out the dimensionality of time, space, contexts, and other forces changing the nature of the reality and the relationship between the brand and the person. They're having a multidimensional life while we're expecting them to follow a very flat and predictable path.

We can do better by allowing experiences to be loosely coupled and connected rather than dependent on a predictable sequence.

We can do better by designing and developing experiences with an awareness of the likely context in which they will be consumed.

We can do better by using data models that capture dimensional information about context and including that in our analysis, so that those considerations become part of future designs.

I call this approach Integrated Human Experience Design[101].

To design in an integrated way across dimensions means to think about how people can experience the same attribute of a brand or company or the same value proposition expressed in different ways in different contexts, interactions, modes, and platforms.

In brief, the elements of Integrated Human Experience Design are:

- Integration (of course)
- Dimensionality
- Metaphors and cognitive associations
- Intentionality/purpose
- Value and emotional load
- Alignment
- Adaptation and iteration

Some of this may sound like a marketing problem, or simply a user experience problem. But it's bigger than that: These are questions of technology deployment, data modeling, and cultural alignment as much as anything else.

On the digital side, when we create e-commerce environments, online banking, online healthcare services, or any website or any mobile app or any API or data system or anything that is going to serve up a digital experience meant to be consumed by humans, we can do so with consideration of the physical environment and context that people are going to be in as they experience those. And that combination of physical environment and context crossed with digital delivery will be more and more diverse all the time; it certainly will not just be screens in offices or homes. Imagine phones and watches everywhere, voice assistants, kiosks on city streets, and even non-interfaces like data being pulled through an API into a connected device.

In a way those wildly varying integrations have a contextlessness and boundarylessness about them that make them challenging to design for. But the key is to focus on making the human experience somewhere along that path as meaningful and dimensional as possible, in alignment with the business objectives you're designing for.

Meaningful Metaphors

❊ ❊ ❊

You start with understanding how a rich understanding of metaphor can lead to the design of exceptional experiences.

Daniel Humm had recently become the executive chef at the New York restaurant Eleven Madison Park when a critic gave a good review but added that it could use "a bit of Miles Davis." This observation made sense to Humm, and he and his team took it to heart.

> After researching "the 11 words that were most often used to describe him," chef Humm and his team made it their mission to make their restaurant reflect those qualities, including: "endless reinvention," "forward-moving," and "collaborative."[102]

Clearly it was not just a literal insight; if that were the case, they could have just piped Miles Davis music in through the speakers and called it a day. But they really thought about what Miles Davis's music means, what the experience of hearing Miles Davis is, what attributes his music has for listeners, and so on, and worked on instilling and infusing those characteristics into the experience to bring it to life through the restaurant.

> So what was once a standard set tasting menu became a grid menu with infinite choices. That format eventually begat a four-hour-plus meal of 16 or more courses. Many of those dishes were elevated riffs on New York's iconic dishes; servers would lift a smoky cloche to reveal buttery slices of sablefish, a nod to the Lower East Side's Jewish appetizing stores. Servers would mix egg cremes tableside with olive oil and sea salt.[103]

It paid off. Eleven Madison Park earned the distinction of the World's Best Restaurant by Eater in 2017.

Another aspect of how metaphors can help with meaning is that they can show nuanced insight into the experience, or the relationship between company and customer in dimensional ways. During the early years at Netflix, when I was working there, the company had its logo redone by an outside agency. It was unveiled at a company meeting. They did the whole thing up; we all had new business cards and everything.

But this new logo design included a rounded square like a TV console, and it incorporated squiggly gray lines, like static running across a TV screen. Most of the employees felt right away that it missed the mark: We felt Netflix was about a love of movies, not about the experience of renting or specifically of watching a movie on your TV at home. Ironically, the metaphor might be closer to true now since we're a lot more accustomed to the experience of watching entertainment at home, and the company's content focuses far more now on traditionally TV-oriented programming (shorter-form and serial). But at the time, the meaningful dimension for the audience was the access to a vast collection of movies they could watch on demand from the comfort of their couch. The ticket stub, the red velvet theater curtain—these were more meaningful metaphors for the experience and more iconic of the brand's value to the subscriber.

Other dominant consumer brands invoke images and associations with sturdiness, balance, strength, resilience, youth, victory, resourcefulness, bucking the status quo, or overcoming physical limitations. The most successful brands then build off of these attributes in every message and every experience. Metaphors are compact containers for a whole lot of meaning.

What you choose to focus on and play up depends on what is significant, relevant, valuable, and meaningful in the relationship between the brand or product and the human using it. Find the meaningful metaphors and dimensions in the brand, the business model, and in the relationship between the business and the human, and then bring them to life.

Extending Metaphor with Meaningful Metadata

When it comes to creating dimensional experiences, there's a great relationship between metaphor and metadata.

The better you can understand the implied metaphors of a brand, the better you can understand how to capture meaningful dimensions of data that reveal how people value it.

Metaphor is about creating a place in someone's brain for them to conceive of the thing you're giving them to do—*as if* it's another thing.

It gives them a whole other set of vocabulary and visual constructs with which to think about that thing.

And metadata is all about how you frame something. We want to have some sense of the data boundaries happening around an experience.

A lot of the discussion of data in this book thus far has been about the kind of data generated by human beings through transactions with systems. Our data trail. But part of what comes along for the ride is the the data inherent to the thing being transacted with — the data that describes the thing. For example, if I watch a video on YouTube, there's data in the fact that I watched that video and when, but there's also the specifications of the video, how long it is, how many people have liked it, its time stamp, and so on.

This metadata is part of the increasing amount of data being collected and connected about us and around us. And this data, and the structure of that data, such as where we go, what we buy, is part of what shapes our experiences.

If you think about the quantified self movement in relation to the modeling of any business for profit maximization, you can start to get a more holistic picture of personal data and its agency and use by us ourselves versus by other entities.

As an experience creator, if that metadata is meaningful in that it aligns with the objectives a person using the service might have and you don't expose it, you're not making the most meaningful use of the metadata. The data you query to populate an experience should align with your brand metaphor and value proposition. The more you understand those dynamics, the greater the power of what you can expose through, say, meaningful search and navigation options.

As you design experiences, you can use data in a way that demonstrates respect to the human and provides insights back to the company about alignment and further opportunities to improve.

Consider Both Nature and Shape of Experiences

"All models are wrong, but some are useful."

—George E. P. Box[104]

A good part of my work examines meaning and meaningful human experience. And I get to analyze, research, write about, and speak about what I discover about the trends and directions that are shaping the future of meaningful human experiences.

One of the things that struck me while writing *Pixels and Place* was the duality to the rapidly changing landscape and yet the largely consistent human needs and instincts relative to it.

So I came up with this model to describe it: nature versus the shape of the experience. It helps us to understand how technologies and design and created experiences—which are all "shapes"—change the context, but the underlying human needs and values—the nature—remain fairly constant.

It's human nature for humans to drink water. But what physical state that water is in, how it's delivered, and how that makes us feel about us and the world is "the shape" of that experience. So we can drink tap water from a glass, or we can bottle that water in thick, heavy glass and label it with a minimalistic, cool typographic logo. The packaging of the water gives a new shape to that experience. It feels aspirational, as if it's telling me I have an opportunity to be better than I am by drinking water this way. But we're still just humans drinking water.

To design dimensionally means to think about how people can experience the same attribute of a brand or the same value proposition expressed in different ways in different contexts, interactions, modes, platforms, etc. So in the context of business change, it may be comforting to know that not everything is changing all the time. It's helpful to think about things in terms of their alignment with human nature, human scale, and human speed. We'll notice that the more an experience seems to align with universal human nature, the more timeless it feels. But the more the experience is driven by a trendy technology, like Snapchat Spectacles, the more volatile that experience feels.

How can you think about that relative to your business offering?

Some of this approach may not always apply in an extended way, but like the George E.P. Box quote, it's a useful model and they're guidelines that can help you remember to bring your planning back to the human experience.

As the shape of our surroundings changes, the shape of our experience changes, too.

This is literal but also metaphorical.

Human experiences do evolve, but the *shapes* change more quickly than the nature. The more you can root your work in nature and meaning, the more it will be steady and consistent and the more people will connect with it.

Much of technology is adding dimensions to our experience. VR/ virtual experiences pop the visual of something into a three-dimensional or multidimensional space. Even ambient data shapes experience.

It's also a helpful model in thinking about transformation, and how we adapt to change.

Game Thinking, Play, and Addictive Versus Benevolent

Gamification

Since about the time Gartner included "gamification" in its 2011 Hype Cycle report on emerging technologies and trends, the world of experience design has been full of ratings, badges, scores, and other bells and whistles designed to keep people coming back for more.

Most likely you have personally experienced the addictive rush or or known people who have been addicted to games like Candy Crush, Angry Birds, Farmville, or World of Warcraft.

Game development companies are often just doing the same things as other companies—seeking local maximums, providing dopamine hits, and enticing people to reach just one more level.

There's an interior design game I often see advertised online—and I've often said that I'd wager it's using a range of human players to train an algorithm, then feeding those results as input to machine learning, and potentially setting up the AI-based decorator of the future.

I can easily imagine using an AI-based service to review my home's interiors and provide recommendations to decorate and furnish it that cater to preferences I specify.

That would probably mean using an embedded camera app to capture a panoramic interior view of my home, of course. So now in this scenario, the app developer has collected images of people's interiors, presumably associated with some personal information. That could set off privacy alarms, and rightly so. (You can read about a similar home data issue raised by the makers of the Roomba in Chapter 28 - Ethics at Scale.)

But play as incentive is nonetheless a big driver of innovation and data gathering.

- Simple ratings, like thumbs up or down
- Swiping right or left, as in popular dating apps like Tinder
- Showing percentage complete, as LinkedIn began doing early on, encouraging people to fill out less-common fields in online profiles

The experience creator can generate a lot of data quickly, but the value of the data is limited to how thoughtfully it represents a meaningful dimension of the experience.

What are the possibilities of benevolent gamification? How could companies, product designers, or experience makers tap into incentives that 1) align with business goals, 2) create more compelling, memorable, share-worthy experiences, and 3) lead to greater human fulfillment?

(Or prioritize them the other way around, because why does human fulfillment always have to be an afterthought?)

On one level, there are brands that integrate actual games into their customer interactions. Take McDonald's and Starbucks, for example. They use games to drive purchase behavior, and as a result they get a more comprehensive picture of the extent of customer willingness, but not of unincentivized behavior that could be maximized.

But there's gamification across the design of all kinds of experiences; it doesn't have to be just games. In some ways, games are the easy design wins, whereas integrating play into non-game applications opens up a world of holistic benefits of increased productivity, increased creativity, and increased integrative thinking.

There's an obvious caution about the flip side: ubiquitous gamification that leads to addictive behaviors, excessive device use, disconnection with humans in our immediate surroundings, etc.

(Not to say connections with humans in virtual space are not relevant and important; they certainly can be. But they aren't necessarily more important than the ones around us, and yet the interfaces can "trick" us into investing more time and energy into those.)

One of the possible unintended consequences of gamifying behavior is that you may get disproportionate participation: Some people overengage while others may be uninterested, and the people who find it addictive may overdo the behavior, leading to skewed results.

In what thoughtful ways can we include gamification in experience design that gets the most relevant cross section of people to participate, gets the participants meaningfully engaged, and doesn't encourage additive behavior?

Can we do this in a way that doesn't contribute to a society where we're disconnected from one another and addicted to the trendy new game?

Some kinds of fitness tracking tools and apps may be one set of examples, such as NikePlus, which offers rewards to users when they are physically active. Even the fitness tracking rings on the Apple Watch are enough to incentivize many people to "get in their steps" for the day.

We could use games, game thinking, gamification, and playful/fun incentives to align human motives with business drivers, using incentives of play to improve intelligence with memory, brain teaser, and meditation apps.

Digital Behavior Change and Digital Transformation

Who among has hasn't heard a ding from our phones and gotten that little dopamine hit? From Facebook and FOMO[105] and instant gratification to Twitter and tl;dr[106]—in all of our digital distraction and shrinking attention spans, have we rewired our brains?

By now you've probably heard of "Dunbar's number," the theoretical limit of meaningful relationships or connections a person can have. It was suggested by British anthropologist Robin Dunbar in the 1990s, and that number is supposed to be 150. The limitation has to do with our cognitive abilities, our ability to maintain complexity, and so on. Dunbar explained it informally as—and I love this explanation —"the number of people you would not feel embarrassed about joining uninvited for a drink if you happened to bump into them in a bar."

You've also probably encountered "online disinhibition effect," even if you didn't know the name for it. This is the role anonymity or even virtual rather than physical presence plays in our online interactions and it accounts for why the guy you know from work who's always so nice in the break room can seem to turn into such a hostile jerk in the comments of a political discussion thread.

The way the Internet has connected us has led to an amazing duality: we have more connections, including sometimes high-quality interactions with people far away from us, *and* we also feel more disconnected from the actuality of people's humanity due to the anonymity of the medium.

The way we engage with some of our normal functions, like eating, shopping, and hanging out with friends, has changed significantly. While experience creators seek our attention, the tradeoff we make when we focus our attention on one form of content or experience is that another experience gets less of our attention. So if we are focused on taking Instagram-ready photos of our meals, for example, we may remember those meals better than if we had not taken the photo, but we may not remember as clearly or connect as deeply with other details of that same dining experience, such as the restaurant decor, or even the people we were with. For us as content consumers, none of this is bad news, exactly; it just demands a certain presence of mind, a certain intentionality of what we choose to engage with, and an awareness of when we might be having experiences for the sake of documenting those experiences.

As experience creators, however, the design of experiences around content, such as with news and other media, is a careful dance between gaining someone's attention and offering them control. What do experience creators and strategists need to think about in the context of this overhaul in people's behavior and appetite for our content and offerings?

As you imagine the context in which someone is consuming your content, say, as a parent listens to a news podcast while driving a child to school, or as a runner listens to music while in a city park, or as someone sits for a few minutes in a coffee shop while reading a story on their tablet, might there be times when you could relinquish control of someone's attention so they may pay closer attention to the people around them and their surroundings?

As you design experiences for scale, part of the consideration is: What are the incentives to the human using the service, buying the product? Can we enrich experiences by designing meaningful incentives for their use and engagement? Just as profit is often too shallow a metric to optimize organizations around, price is often a terrible incentive for inspiring customer behavior, and yet it's often the default. Sometimes convenience, another default, is enough of an incentive, but it's worth digging deeper and considering if there may be other facets of the experience that align the evolving digital experience with deeper human motivations, such as the joy of sharing a new discovery with other people, the warmth of being appreciated for loyalty, or the richness of fostering a human relationship.

As companies learn to adjust to evolving and emerging business models that increasing rely on data, automation, algorithms, and various kinds of artificial intelligence, they will also need to adapt to the way humans adapt to these contexts.

CHAPTER 30

A "Tech Humanist" Approach to Machine-Led Human Experiences

I'M EXCITED TO INTRODUCE THIS enhanced version of my framework for Integrated Human Experience Design that is intended for enriching automated or machine-led human experiences. Introducing Automated IHED: Automated Integrated Human Experience Design.

The overall principles that we'll explore further in this chapter are:

- Don't Just Automate the Menial; Automate the Meaningful
- Automate Empathy
- Use Human Data Respectfully
- Reinvest Gains into Humanity and Human Experiences

It's fundamentally the design of algorithmic experiences, while giving major consideration for what the outlier experiences are likely to look like at scale. Imagine all the ways you can think of that the interactions and experiences could lead the user astray, could be frustrating, confusing, disappointing, misleading, painful, triggering, etc.

In other words, start with simple if-then statements in how the process is supposed to work, but work to find the nuance beyond the if-then statements. If-then statements don't really require machine learning. Add nuance.

The typical approach to deciding what and how to automate is based on cost savings, revenue maximization, and profit optimization. Those are all incredibly important drivers of business success, but they are missing the dimension of human success that takes into account factors like impact, alignment, relevance, meaning, purpose, and loyalty.

In reality, the practical outcomes may often be the same. But the little nuances of interactions, feature labeling, messaging, alignment with internal processes and operations, and measurement of success will make incremental adjustments possible that steer the business toward profit while creating as meaningful an experience for the human as possible.

In the simplest forms of automation, we may have a manual process and replace a step with software or hardware.

Design for alignment with your business model. You're looking for product design that, like Amazon Prime, furthers both business and customer objectives. I don't think most companies should try to be like Amazon or Uber in most ways, but in terms of operationalizing the business around digital touchpoints and integrated products, they are useful examples. At its most fundamental this is not about *digital* transformation; this is about *business* transformation, using strategic product design and then modeling it with data and digital interactions to drive behavior that aligns and furthers both business and customer objectives.

Don't Just Automate the Menial; Automate the Meaningful

So often we hear the idea that we should automate the menial, the meaningless, the tedious to free humans up to focus on higher-level work, higher-level thought and activities, and higher-level living. And of course, to accelerate productivity for profit.

I won't deny that the idea sounds lovely in theory. But if you follow that thought to scale and imagine a world where most of our surroundings are, to some degree, automated, where our lives are increasingly augmented by technology, where more and more human interactions are replaced by machines, it becomes more clear that if we only automated what was menial, we would soon find ourselves surrounded by meaningless, rudimentary, rote, reductive interactions with devices and machines that have no awareness of our human emotional needs, no allowance for context.

> If we only automated what was menial, we would soon find ourselves surrounded by meaningless, rudimentary, rote, reductive interactions.

It makes sense to automate routine, menial tasks. Machines tend to be faster and more reliable at repetitive work anyway. But in addition to that imperative, we should identify the meaningful elements in the interactions we develop for humans to have with machines, and look for ways to amplify that meaning. Many of our experiences are increasingly so data-driven that we must push ourselves to think about data in an more meaningful and dimensional way.

Further, if you imagine the world where more and more human tasks become automated, and human work is gradually augmented and eventually displaced and replaced by automation, we find ourselves in a new situation. So much of our sense of meaning has traditionally come from work, from our accomplishments, from our sense of contribution to society, from our feeling of providing for ourselves and our families.

So in that more automated world, to make up for what we'll lose when work becomes more automated, we will need more meaning in our lives: an ambient, embedded sense of meaning that must be built and encoded now into the soon-to-be heavily automated world around us.

Besides, everything that makes creating meaningful experiences in business successful applies even more so when we apply those principles to automated experiences.

"That makes sense," people have said when I point this out. "But how on earth can you automate meaning?"

Perhaps the words seem contradictory. To many people I talk with, the very idea of an automatic, programmed action sounds like something that couldn't possibly involve meaning, purpose, intention, or empathy.

But the programming that defines the way automation operates is inherently based on some some sense of what's important, and some understanding of rules that follows from that. That's why the business objectives that compel that automation must be tied to a clear sense of purpose. It's informed by everything that the rest of this book lays out: Every time a company's purpose drives its experience design, every time a data model takes context into account, every time we can appreciate the dimensional feeling of a brand interaction, we are that much closer to being surrounded by experiences that are rich rather than reductive.

How could automation relate to your purpose and the meaningful experience of the humans who interact with your company?

What does it look like to build meaning into automation? It means allowing for relevance, context, using things like location awareness and state awareness to make your user/consumer's life easier, as well as to align experience more with company/entity goals. It means designing for dimensionality.

There's going to continue to be a need for the human-to-human, no question about it. But even more importantly, there will continue to be a need for the human capability to understand meaning and nuance all throughout experience design, whether the experience is conducted by a human or a machine.

Again, humans tend to do nuance well, so some of the work for humans to do in getting our society ready for more and more automation is to think holistically and humanistically about the context in which people will encounter these automated experiences, then try to inject some awareness of purpose and some sense of empathy for the person. That will take many forms, and some of the differences made will be very subtle, such as handling an error message with a little more grace. But when you magnify those subtle differences across the scale we're eventually talking about, it could make for a significantly different—and better—world.

The pace of technology is accelerating, and along with it the apparent pace of business and our lives. We need to accept the promise of technology and let it help us do more with less. The alternative is too stubborn, too arrogant, too resistant to the tidal wave of change already sweeping culture and human behavior.

Automate Empathy

One of the steps to automating for meaningful experience is to design those experiences for empathy. Starting with empathy for the human need that goes into the interaction gives you tremendous advantages in being able to find alignment with your business objective, and tremendous opportunity to create meaningful experiences at scale.

Do we need to know whether the agent we're interacting with is human or machine? (See Should a Bot Have to Tell You It's a Bot for more.)

Think of how this plays out in the context of a customer support center. The business purpose of a customer support center is to resolve obstacles to customer continuation, to reduce cancellations of service, and to reinforce the shared values of the company and the customer for greatest chance of customer longevity and loyalty (which is more profitable than losing a customer).

What purpose does the human on the other side of the transaction have, or what intention? The person reaching out to the call center wants to solve a problem, to vent, to have grievances redressed, and to feel heard and understood and appreciated as a customer.

Your best bet at creating an empathetic experience here, automated or not, is to genuinely hear the customer's issue, resolve it quickly, and ultimately to note the pattern of successful resolution for future instances that resemble this instance.

Or let's say you're a bank, and a customer is reaching out about a problem about their account.

To date, customer support phone trees have typically not been empathetic. The ones that attempt to interpret voice instructions may do better. Let's hope chatbots and other emerging automation can do better too.

The least empathetic approach is a routine "press 1 for x, press 2 for y, press * to hear these options again."

Provide an option for humans to deal with humans. Sometimes we humans just need to feel heard.

Chatbots and other automated systems succeed at making customers feel like they can accomplish what they need to do most efficiently, as long as they know what they need to do and the task is fairly straightforward, like changing an account password.

But the moment the task requires understanding and complex support, customers lose confidence that automated systems will be able to help them, and a human agent begins to look like the more empathetic option.

In a manufacturing environment, the business purpose is efficient production for a profitable sale. The function of the human on the other side of the transaction is to assure quality, low price/fair price.

(But then there is a certain added value to human-made goods. So if your manufacturing environment is, in fact, human-made and small-batch, why not label a product as "Made by humans with love"?)

In a retail environment, the business function is to sell goods at a reasonably predictable rate. The function of the human on the other side of the transaction is finding what you need versus discovery.

I wrote in *Pixels and Place* about some of the trends shaping retail in terms of digital integration, such as smart mirrors and smart fitting rooms. What we can see about the future of retail in a Tech Humanist context? Mixed reality shopping environments, home delivery partly through autonomous vehicles and drones, and customization on unprecedented levels.

For more about supply chain transparency, see the section on Supply Chain, IoT Sensors, Automation, Other Tech Impacts on Operations.

Use Human Data Respectfully

Business will collect people's data as a matter of transacting with them anyway. Our guiding principle in business should be to use people's data to treat them more respectfully as human beings. Let their data guide you toward their intentions and how they align with your business purpose. Don't overreach, don't use data intrusively, and guard it with respect.

Analytics are people. The vast majority of all this data is human data. It's us: you and me and everyone we know, moving through the world, making purchases, interacting with each other, interacting with devices and brands, communicating, considering, and consuming.

Relevance is a form of respect. Once you acknowledge that business data *is* people, it becomes clear that creating relevant experiences from that data to guide people seamlessly to information and products that solve their problems can be treated as a form of respect. Seeking a resolution that aligns business objectives and human objectives is the only way to marry sustainable business success, ethics, and a hopeful future for humanity. We cannot forget that we are all human.

Discretion is a form of respect, too. Targeting is a big opportunity in business, but if you don't think through the ramifications of demonstrating what you know, you could come off as creepy.

Protect human data excessively. Protect the human data you collect. Invest in cybersecurity systems. Make sure your own business policies treat that data with respect. Don't forget that your data, too, is being handled by companies all over the world, so we must *all* treat *all* human data with respect. Treat it as if it were your own, because it is.

Reinvest Gains into Humanity and Human Experiences

I propose that for every way that your business gains efficiency through automation, you look to invest some of those gains in human resources and human development. Look for opportunities to make the human experiences of your customers and your employees more meaningful, and look for opportunities to have humans on your staff and as part of your culture bringing human value to the process.

It is also worth exploring how your offering can reach and engage with humans without need for exchange of money.

CHAPTER 31

Scale for Meaningful Experiences

PERHAPS IT IS BECAUSE WE ourselves are things that grow that we tend to deem growth good.

But growth can get out of hand. Ask anyone who's battled cancer. Or just anyone who's tried to fit into their jeans from high school.

Surely not all growth is good. And in a business context, not all growth is proportional. Growth occurs along one dimension, like revenue. You can quickly let one facet of the business overtake the ability of the business to keep up. Scale, in theory, is what happens when you grow along multiple dimensions, proportionally.

But even scale sometimes has unintended consequences.

Normally when we talk about scale in terms of start-ups or corporate growth, we're talking about removing hard limits so that growth opportunities can expand in terms of multiples, like 3x, 5x, or hey, even 10x.

But in thinking about automation, artificial intelligence, and other machine-led growth, we're talking about the fullness of what happens when a notion meets *exponential* expansion possibility.

That's what happens when data can model it, and software can accelerate it, and automation can amplify it, and culture can adopt it.

What we need to realize is that whatever we automate probably will scale; and it will scale like never before.

In that sense, for the Tech Humanist approach to work, we need to carefully consider every one of our strategic and design decisions. Ask: How would this work at scale?

Humanity at Scale, and How We Automate The Best Of Us

I'm fairly obsessed with the challenge of adapting experiences to scale: puzzling to figure out what an experience will do at scale, what unintended consequences it might have for the people who interact with it, or on its surroundings or on culture.

My focus on this is because it is increasingly clear that what is automated will scale; it will scale like never before. So we need to focus on scaling the right things.

How will humanity itself scale? By scale, I don't mean grow in population. That's already underway, and the consequences of that growth are troubling. If anything, overpopulation is an example of growth out of proportion, not in scale, because as it stands, the resources and infrastructure don't keep up. No, what I mean is how will humanity's characteristics, its promise, its values, its bright future scale?

I'm not overlooking the badness and baggage of humanity, too. We've got a history of wars, slavery, colonies, greed, and Twitter trolling. Yes, the behavior in online spaces can be as brutal and savage as anything out of antiquity.

All of that exists, and it's why our technology deployments and data models need to be built around our best inclinations. We can't allow the worst of human behavior to be the guide for artificially-intelligent automation that determines human experiences.

The fact is, we encode our biases into data, into algorithms, into technology as a whole. Machines are what we encode of our human selves.

* * *

Machines are what we encode of our human selves.

As we develop an increasingly machine-driven future, with every new development or update, we get the chance to encode the best of who we are: our best intentions rather than our basest instincts. We could infuse the future with our brightest hope, our most egalitarian views, our most evolved understandings.

And the data strategy we develop has to account for this as well. Our data models must include useful, meaningful human interactions and must optimize for incentives beyond profit: wellness, equity, sustainability. Ultimately, business success relies on human success.

We need to examine how data and tech shape our experiences, so we can embrace the future with possibility rather than paranoia.

Machine-driven experiences really are gaining momentum, and automation really is accelerating in ways that are bigger than us. Data-driven, machine-scaled systems are—or will soon be—literally creating the world around us.

Job displacement and replacement by automation will occur, and we don't yet know exactly what that will mean for the future of human work. Digital systems will determine our lives and our fates, so it's in our best interest as humans to think through now what we're building and scaling around us.

Algorithms will keep leapfrogging algorithms, so especially when you put algorithms and logic in place to optimize transactions around some metric or data point, when you let machine learning systems take a crack at it, scale takes on a whole new level of importance.

And that's exciting, but it also means we need to carefully consider every one of our strategic and design decisions—especially the things we automate or may automate in the future (which at some point is almost everything) — from the standpoint of "how would this work at scale"?

When you're going to be creating a moment where you — or a proxy of you — interacts with another person — or a proxy of another person, what makes that meaningful? A starting point for answering that is to think about the purpose the interaction supports. One way or the other, it's clear we're going to need all the sophistication we can get to think about building purpose into automation.

Because if it's not done from a place of organizational strategic purpose and alignment you might end up with some unintended consequences. It will grow and it might even scale because it will pull resources along with it but sometimes with that kind of scale, if not done from a place of centralized organizational purpose and alignment, you might have unintended consequences.

Some things become absurd at scale.

My focus is on meaningful human experiences; and the natural opposite of meaningful experiences is absurd experiences.

So as a starting place for infusing the best and most meaningful attributes of humanity into technology, we can start by not giving absurdity a chance to scale.

Don't let absurdity get in there. It's like a weed; it will just grow and spread, and if you ever try to get it out it will be. And the thing about absurdity is once it's been there a while we stop even noticing that it's there, but we also stop noticing what we're not seeing, and what could be there instead.

Part of the challenge is a lack of integration: We have traditionally drawn boundaries around the concepts of art and commerce. Art was pure creative expression: connecting with some kind of human truth. And commerce was all about transactions: selling goods and services. As various kinds of technology grew into an experience infrastructure around us, we have more or less relegated technological development to the world of commerce, assuming transactional interests would optimize them for us.

The problem with this dichotomy is the disconnect and dehumanization of business motives left unchecked by human interests. And moreover, this dichotomy has been sliced through in every imaginable way: with sponsored content, advertorials, edutainment, and data informing all manner of creative and entertainment services.

Since technology-driven commercial experineces integrate with our surroundings more and more, we need rich thinking on what kind of human values they model, and what kinds of human purpose they support.

We can ask:

- How will this experience impact culture at scale?
- How will this experience impact brand at scale?
- What is the purpose of the experience we're rolling out?
- How will we measure its success?
- What will happen in our business if this particular experience/product/campaign is successful beyond our wildest dreams? (For example, there may be exaggerated costs of supporting a product, say, an accessory line, that was only meant to be superfluous. You might even feel the need to pivot the business to focus on that product as the core.) Are we prepared to support that possibility?
- What will happen if it flops?
- For whom is this the most useful? Is that the user segment we most want to connect with?

The more you think from purpose through the human experience at scale, the less you risk scaling absurd, unintended consequences.

Scale for More Meaningful Business Objectives

Jim Collins's business classic *Good to Great* is a must-read anyway, but especially the bit on the Hedgehog concept and the profit-per-x denominator[107]: as he puts it, what drives your "economic engine."

Even though Collins is talking about "cash flow" per X or "profit" per X, this philosophy of understanding what makes your business tick is bigger than cash or profit. Note that the metric is not merely profit. It's a dimensional understanding of profit; it's how that profit fits into a bigger mechanism, a more holistic understanding of the model.

As we scale into the Tech Humanist future, we need to look for business objectives more dimensional than profit, and models more meaningful than advertising.

There's also the consideration of factors beyond an obvious monetary incentive: environmental sustainability, for example; or the empowerment of more people in turbulent economic conditions who in turn may empower others and help pull them out of economic risk. Common sense tells us the world becomes kinder, not to mention probably safer, the less we leave others in jeopardy.

Besides, there are valid business models to be built around holistically rewarding ideas. Take thredUP, for instance, an online secondhand clothing store. With all of the user conventions of regular online fashion retail, they have quickly become a dominant retailer, offering affordable designer brands to fashionistas willing to wear previously owned clothes, compensating people for the used clothes they send in to be sold, and keeping unwanted clothes out of landfills.

These questions have global impact. So for those of us who have grown up knowing the United States as not only a military superpower but also a commercial one, when it comes to scale, we have to sit with the question: How do emerging global powers (such as China) shape the trajectory of automation and humanity?

Y Combinator, the start-up incubator and accelerator that helped to launch hundreds of companies such as Airbnb, Dropbox, Instacart, and more, announced in August 2018 that they are launching in China. Alibaba, a Chinese-based conglomerate and the world's largest retailer, is a huge force globally, as are companies like Tencent and Baidu. Just the scale of human population living in China means that technologies successfully serving that demographic are already global forces.

Possibly an even bigger question is: How do we develop human-centric technologies in cultures where human values differ from our own?

When Saudi Arabia granted citizen status to Sophia the robot, Twitter was rife with sardonic jokes about the robot having more rights than women in Saudi Arabia, a country known for denying equal rights to women. After all, "she" accepted her citizenship without wearing a headscarf and without being accompanied by a male guardian. Since the robot was made by a Hong Kong based company, "she" is also a foreigner, and Saudi Arabia also doesn't typically grant citizenship to foreigners.

How does North Korea's presence on the global political scene influence the realities of scaling technologies? Or any aspiring dictator?

In any discussion of global trade, global policy-making, and cultural relations, we need sincere consideration of these questions.

Because nuclear powers are a form of technology, to be sure. And AI-powered military robots will be quite another.

One way or the other, it's clear that there are bigger issues on the horizon than just profitability. It's time for business models to include reflection on integrated impacts as we grow them to scale.

Don't Let Absurdity Scale

In January 2018 in Seattle, on a chilly Monday morning, a cashier-less checkout concept store called Amazon Go opened to the public. The shelves were stocked with normal grocery items, and at first glance you might have thought it looked like any other grocery store. But instead of waiting in a line for the registers to ring up and pay, customers just took what they'd picked up off the shelves and walked out.

An array of cameras and sensors associated products with the customers who picked them up. The store tallied up the totals, and the payments happened in the accompanying app.

It's all quite seamless and exciting, as new experiences go. Of course it raises immediate questions about the long-term consequences of replacing human cashier jobs—the same questions that arise from every other kind of automation that displaces a human function. We'll come back to that below. We have covered much on automation, but in the scope of this chapter, we need to examine other consequences, too, in terms of how values and meaning amplify when data and technology are used to scale human experience.

When you launch the Amazon Go app, you get a step-by-step overview of how the process works, how payment happens, and so on.

You know how sometimes you might stop and pick up something for someone else? Maybe like me, you're tall and can reach the top shelf, or maybe someone can't bend over to reach the low shelf and you can. That's very nice of you. But you just got charged for their purchase.

In order to charge shoppers automatically, the system assigns the purchase to the shopper who picks up the item—which makes sense in most scenarios. But if one shopper helps another reach a product, the helper will be charged instead.

Screen shots from the Amazon Go app

Certainly this specific problem may be easy to fix and may be resolved by the time this book goes to print. But the point is, any time you change the usual shape of experience, you risk running counter to the cultural assumptions and associations that go with it. And you risk scaling absurd unintended consequences.

Scale can exacerbate even small amounts of absurdity. The Amazon Go "just walk out" experience is elegant on one hand, but it relies on automating the act of noticing on the other; and the way it achieves the feat, which is through an array of cameras and sensors furiously calculating what has been picked up and to whom it belongs, requires intricate and complex technology compared to the perceived simplicity of how humans notice and observe (even though that system probably requires a lot of complexity deeper down).

The absurdity comes from accommodating that complexity and how it challenges our usual methods of experiencing shopping. After all, experience at scale shapes culture. It just does. Because experience at scale *is* culture.

> Experience at scale shapes culture.
>
> Experience at scale *is* culture.

So we need to be mindful of the bigger picture of human experiences when we are developing strategy and deploying technology to satisfy a business need.

Experiencing Absurdity at Scale

The bike sharing company ofo stood to introduce exciting, innovative changes in US markets by being one of the first companies to launch dockless bike sharing, meaning that riders would not be restricted in their usage of the bikes by the locations and availability of docking spaces around a city. The bikes unlock through an app that scans a QR code on the bike and checks it out to the user's account, and then locks it again when the user marks the ride as completed so that in theory, the bikes could be left anywhere.

And everywhere. And so they have been.

In some cities, the overwhelming impression residents have of the brand, as well as competing brands like Spin and Mobike, is that the bikes are clutter. Residents find them strewn around the sidewalks. That has led to measures such as the one in Dallas, whose city council passed regulations in June 2018 requiring companies to seek permits and pay the city per bike or scooter.

The same phenomenon has been happening with sharing-economy-enabled electric scooters in certain markets, such as Bird and Lime. Nashville and other cities clamped down on scooter companies like Bird for the chaos they were causing in the city, between the scooters littering the sidewalks and the precarious effect on the foot traffic in the street or on busy sidewalks. Nashville's city council eventually passed regulations that re-allowed the scooters but capped the number of scooters each company could have in the city, as well as rider guidelines and other restrictions.

The upshot is that people now have a negative impression of some of these brands when they hear the name. They think not of the benefits—which are considerable in cities exactly like Dallas and Nashville, where population growth and infrastructure challenges make multimodal mobility and flexibility solutions sorely needed—but instead of the hassles associated with the lack of structure and the absurdity of the experience at scale.

Experience at scale shapes brand.

For Whose Future Is an Innovation Like Amazon Go?

We have to ask: For whom is Amazon Go a benefit? Most people looking at it would start by observing it's bad news for cashiers if those jobs go away. But a reasonable counter-question is: Does it create new, different jobs in data entry and inventory/records management? This is why the human experience perspective is necessary, rather than solely looking at *customer* experience or *user* experience. The focus on the specific role of *customer* experience allows us to overlook the *human* experience of those who occupy the role of *employee*. It's fair and worthwhile from the context of the business to optimize for efficiency, but at some level of scale, there needs to be a reckoning with how that business model squares with humanity and how it contributes to human outcomes.

It's all too easy for intelligent automation and the scale that comes with it to have disproportionate benefits and not only reinforce but widen existing wealth inequality — those who have money to invest will make exponentially more money. The haves get even more; the have-nots get even less.

The answer is, I hope obviously, not *not* to innovate. The answer is bound to be more integrative, more "both/and" than that. We can *both* embrace emerging technologies and the benefits of intelligent automation *and* ensure that the full range of people impacted are part of our thought process and design considerations. It's a challenge that goes with the territory, but it takes meaningful consideration of the full experience, nature, shape, and impact to create the best futures for the most people.

Collect Data for Aligned Purposes

While collecting data is important for innovation, and while a wide range of data may be required to dimensionalize experiences and scale them effectively, companies should only be collecting the human data that models aligned intentions and objectives.

As I wrote in *Pixels and Place*, a 2016 article in the *Independent* reported that Uber collects battery level information from users calling for rides. As a result, they know when your phone is about to die.[108] Through experiments, they also know that you're more likely to pay "surge" fares as a result. In the same article, the company representative states that Uber has not rolled any such feature into live production. But in collecting data that lends itself to manipulation rather than aligned outcomes, they impose an ethical burden on themselves.

Companies and experience creators must find ways to accelerate innovation without setting themselves up to exploit human data or to breach people's trust. Human data should be collected in alignment with what the human anticipates from the outcome.

The upshot is: Data is not inherently evil, and collecting data for the purpose of maximizing the experience is part of business. But it's human data, and business objectives need to align with the human intentions that give over that data.

Optimizing Experiences with Algorithms and AI

Algorithms and AI are going to maximize what we design them to do. So rather than the model that has long dominated business where we opportunistically maximize incentives for what in many cases are human weaknesses where they intersect with business interests, we face the imperative to alter our approach, knowing that business drivers are likely to scale like never before, and knowing that scale sometimes has unintended consequences.

Algorithms *opportunities* **Figuring Out Where/How is Effective to Automate** *insights*

Automation Opportunistically Simulating and Maximizing Human Motivation at Scale

Rather than opportunistically optimizing behavior and motives for profit, we can figure out where and how we can meaningfully automate, and then use automation to meaningfully simulate and maximize human value at scale for aligned success.

As we've discussed, it's not that you shouldn't automate; but wherever possible, automate the meaningful.

Automate the meaningful.

What does that look like in practice? Automating the meaningful looks like finding the meaning in human interactions and amplifying it. It looks like identifying ways to develop automation and AI that improve with human input and feedback for nuance and context.

Humans Figuring Out Where/How is Meaningful to Automate

opportunities

Automation Meaningfully Simulating and Maximizing Human Value at Scale

insights

This is an opportunity to answer two questions simultaneously:

How can we scale business meaningfully through strategic alignment and automation?

and

How can we create meaningful experiences and scale them through data and automation?

AI will require empathy and all the meaningful experience and alignment to do marketing for humans. Just because it's automated or accruing machine intelligence doesn't mean it doesn't need human strategy, course correction, and more. As long as you're hoping to influence humans, human advisory will always have value.

From there, we can use data and technology to scale what is meaningful.

What can you do in business that legitimately uses AI to solve business problems and human problems? Recommendations engines, speech recognition, spam/troll filtering, comment moderation, community management, fraud detection, and more.

Any problem in business with a good data set, plenty of examples, a lot of variability, and direct feedback is a good candidate for a machine learning approach.

Using Robots and Automation to Scale Human Experiences

When most of us think about robots, we tend to picture either Rosie from *The Jetsons* or the Terminator. But robots have been around for decades in various forms, some helping out on manufacturing floors, and some allowing biotech and electronics cleanrooms to be safer and more sanitary by augmenting human actions. Some are even children's toys.

Don't forget virtual robots: software programs that can adapt and respond to input and provide assistance and interactions in real time, in digital and/or virtual space. We already have virtual assistants of various kinds, such as x.ai, which primarily assists with calendars and scheduling, or Trim, which assists with managing spending and bills. A rumored product called Google Coach would even provide AI-powered workout and meal plan recommendations[109]. And many of us are getting more and more familiar with voice interactions.

All of that is leading to converging experiences and automation — voice and virtual assistants, like Apple's Siri or Amazon's Alexa, but also the emerging Google assistant that imitates humanlike pauses in speech. (Refer back to Human Imitation by Machines.) That space is still new, and more innovation is still to come.

As business works to achieve its objectives at scale, automation becomes inevitable. Some of the challenge, then, is to automate sensibly, to invest in human skills training, and to make sure people are prepared to take on the higher-level tasks that come with greater deployment of automation.

For more on this, have a look at the section on Robotic Process Automation.

CHAPTER 32

Deploy Relevant Technology: A Playbook

THE BIGGEST OPPORTUNITY OF ALL for accelerating business purpose to market is deploying relevant technology that streamlines how the company interacts with people who are users and customers of the product or service.

That can happen in various ways, and the shape of that technology mix will almost always be changing.

Purpose helps you understand that you're trying to achieve an outcome beyond the limited scope of the technology deployment so you can progress from, say, a website interaction to a mobile interaction to a wearable interaction to a conversational interaction.

But with so many kinds of technologies emerging all the time, it can be impossible to keep up with which ones are really gaining traction and usage, as well as which technologies make sense to invest in for your company.

This section is intended to give you tools of inspiration: a chance to consider emerging technologies through the lens of purpose and see what they have to offer you and the humans two whom you provide products and services. I think of the opportunity as being a little like Brian Eno's "Oblique Strategies," which are a set of creative prompts that challenge the writer or artist to consider their work in a different way. We'll explore some of the technologies that show the most promise of making a lasting impact, and how to think of them in relation to your brand, your product, your customers' intention, and your purpose.

We'll look at the technologies themselves—such as augmented reality, virtual reality, wearables, the artificial intelligence space, automation, robots, and beyond—and review some of the trends and approaches that employ them. You can use this tool with your teams to spark new ideas for creating more meaningful experiences for the humans who do business with your company and your brand.

If you are making decisions on behalf of a business about what emerging technologies to invest in, I want to help you make the right decisions and drive your business forward. Increasingly, these kinds of technologies are table stakes in business. I also want to encourage you to think in a purpose-driven, aligned, human-centric way with these technologies.

Each of these technologies, platforms, and approaches can be combined to make solutions that work for your business, in your environment, for your customers and constituents, and help us achieve the vision of making experiences better for the most people.

This section will be updated and expanded in an interactive supplement available at techhumanistbook.com.

The Adaptive Future

The technologies of the adaptive future are about allowing for variance and keeping up with change.

The term "adaptive technology" often refers to a range of tools and solutions that enhance the capabilities of people with disabilities. In the context of digital transformation and uses of technology for the best futures for the most people, we can include that set of tools and expand beyond it. It is not uncommon, at any rate, that in designing solutions that suit people with disabilities or for broader use than just the one we first think of, we come up with superior experiences for the majority of humans. Curb cuts at intersections for wheelchair accessibility make it easier to drag a handcart or a suitcase over, as well. Closed captioning for people with hearing loss turns out to be a useful feature to enable online if you want to get the gist of videos with the sound turned off. The OXO Good Grips brand of kitchen utensils was initially designed for people with arthritis and other difficulties with grip, but their ease of use turned out to have such wide appeal that they sustained an annual growth rate over 30 percent for a decade[110]. Inclusive design tends to be adaptive, and adaptive design will get us where we need to go.

Adaptive learning is a major trend in education, often involving some combination of open tools and frameworks, big data, and machine learning that analyzes the learner's responses and behavior and optimizes the subsequent steps and learning pathways based on predicted best likelihood of successful outcomes.

Cybersecurity models built around adaptive responses to evolving threats are growing in popularity, as well. Rather than a control-and-ownership-based approach to authentication and asset protection, emerging platforms are using machine learning, blockchain, and a variety of other tools to stay a step ahead of security risks.

Augmented Reality for Decision-Making, Enjoyment, Learning

The big opportunity for business in thinking about possible futures is to think about how some aspect of their offering could be useful, engaging, or fun in some other context for people.

Augmented reality had a big moment in the summer of 2016 when Pokémon GO! came out, and for a few weeks it seemed like the whole world was playing. But since that craze died down, nothing in the AR space has made such a big splash.

It seems inevitable, though: There's so much potential in this technology.

Augmented reality is getting a lot of play in the form of filters for photos in apps like Snapchat and Facebook.

Think of it as layers—a layer of one context over another. It could be a context of entertainment overtopping your surroundings, a la Pokémon GO!, or it could be a layer of reference information, a video call with a friend, sports scores, or whatever overtops the screen you're primarily using for another function.

How can a virtual layer of data and experience overtopping a "real" or physical layer enhance the connection between your business objectives and the human objectives?

IKEA was already experimenting with augmented reality as early as 2013, with AR integrations with the annual product catalog that let catalog browsers peek "inside" furniture in the catalog photos. That was engaging, playful, and a good way to get some press coverage.

But they now have a far more Tech Humanist approach.

Using AR Kit, a toolkit made by Apple for developing augmented reality applications on iOS devices, IKEA built an app called IKEA Place that lets customers imagine the store's furniture in their own homes.

They also use an image recognition engine to let the app's users take a photo of something they like, and the app will match it to the closest existing item in the product catalog.

All of this is only useful if it aligns your business objectives with the objectives of the humans who do business with you, and you just about couldn't get more aligned than what's happening with IKEA Place.

Placing furniture in your home doesn't have the same impact to humanity as, say, curing cancer. But not every experience has to be profound to be meaningful in some way. If it contributes to a better quality of life for people, and if it helps them accomplish what they need to in a way that makes them feel less anxious, less confused, or less conflicted, then it's arguably a worthwhile use of technology.

Perhaps your business or organizational challenge isn't represented by a product catalog. Is there another kind of overlay people can use? Can you help them make some kind of decision in as close to a real world setting for them as possible?

There are huge opportunities for augmented reality in a classroom setting. For example, students could interact with examples of architecture or geology.

A helpful resource you can download is the IDEO and Google Play collaboration on Human-Centered Design Prompts for Emerging Technologies[111] (link in footnotes). It's a set of twenty "deliberations, considerations, and provocations" that can guide you through some of the strategic possibilities for a variety of platforms and tools.

The Tech Humanist approach to this kind of integrative brand experience with augmented reality or any other kind of adaptive technology is about creating or approximating the context a person will be in when they decide whether yours is the product or service that solves their problem or enhances their life in some way.

The Responsive Future

The technologies of the responsive future also include environments that respond to us. We've all seen movies with billboards that adapt to the person passing near them. Those exist now, as you may be aware, and they're just the beginning of a whole suite of technologies that can change messaging, form, and more depending on who is nearby, how they're consuming the content, and more. If you take a moment to picture that type of technology at scale—and I mean, you don't have to imagine anything remotely as garish or overwhelming as Times Square to get the picture—it should be abundantly obvious why an overarching principle of serving humanity's best interest should be central to the design of these environments.

It may be easy to confuse adaptive and responsive. The key difference between them is that *adaptive* is design for anticipated variances in human behavior and circumstances, whereas *responsive* experiences adjust as needed. If you're familiar with the concept of web design being either adaptive or responsive, the difference is typically understood to be that adaptive designs are optimized for set sizes of screens, whereas responsive designs adjust to the size of the browser at any point. There are advantages to either approach, depending on the design considerations at hand, just as there are advantages to thinking about emerging technology solutions in an adaptive or a responsive context—or both, as needed.

Doors that open and close automatically as a person approaches or walks away are a familiar form of responsive environment in a public space, even though they've been around for a long time.

Future experiences may adjust to the people encountering them by via sensors, interaction with robots, ambient fixtures through gestures, or wearables to detect proximity, temperature, or any kind of movement.

Smart Cities and Responsive Environments

A great many of the innovations already happening in "smart cities" would probably strike people as boring, or at least invisible. These are improvements relating to areas such as utilities, power grids, and traffic flow.

While these improvements certainly do help improve citizens' quality of life, they aren't really noticeable and they don't *feel* responsive.

What are the ways smart and responsive cities could help people thrive? First, let's note the difference between smart cities and responsive cities. The first smart city initiatives were about technology deployments like fixed sensors all over the place. But at this point, human movement through cities with smartphones and other devices provides a far more compelling mesh for experience design and optimization. The trend is now moving away from technology-centric and sensor-centric to being driven more by the data generated by citizens on the move. In other words, more human-centric.

Bike share programs, whether based on docking the bikes with each ride or a dockless program, are heavily dependent on data, algorithms, and sensors; they are also wildly responsive to the ebb and flow of people who use them. Throughout the day, support teams move and reallocate bikes from heavy drop-off centers to in-demand pickup centers.

The solutions that respond to human needs in real time create almost an Augmented Reality layer of sorts for the city.

The questions are: What is the emphasis in smart cities? What are they optimizing for?

The rush to fulfill the requirements of the Amazon selection process for a second headquarters, or HQ2, resulted in 238 cities bidding and a wave of discussions about how most cities would see questionable returns from such an investment[112]. Some said cities would be better off without it and would create more jobs by investing in a start-up ecosystem, diversifying their bets over many smaller companies rather than pooling their resources into one massive employer[113].

Again the Tech Humanist question comes back to what an organization — or city — is trying to do at scale.

A good deal of what happens in smart cities is about "back office" city management more than about providing interactive apps for city denizens. Not that this isn't important, but there's also tremendous opportunity to use technology to make public spaces more usable and human-centric with digital public spaces, smart and responsive city technologies, and responsive built environments. Just as the introduction of public green space in cities increases quality of life, the right kinds of digital and integrated tools and services can allow people to live and breathe.

Citizens can share access[114] to spaces, tools, and other belongings[115].

If we believe internet access as a utility is an increasingly important human right, smart city initiatives might include something as "low tech" and simple as providing WiFi and connected services.

The more ambient data is tracked and used to adjust the space, the more it stands to improve the quality of life. But of course, that's our human data we're talking about, so it has to be done with care and respect.

Open data and open government initiatives can help improve human life at scale through collecting data that allows cities to provide better optimized services — such as collecting suggestions, ideas, and information from citizens, and even crowdsourcing information, feedback, and statistics on accessibility, safety, etc. In some cases, the value can go further by combining these efforts with data from private enterprise.

There's tremendous public value in using data to study disaster relief impact, flood maps[116], air quality, traffic and congestion, sustainable energy, and noise pollution.

How do we make these environments responsive to human needs, in a way parallel to the idea of web design that responds to the screen in which it is viewed?

This topic overlaps heavily with the focus of *Pixels and Place*, so I have only touched on it here, and only as it relates to technology to scale meaningful experiences and best futures for most people. If integrated environments are of interest to you and the projects you are undertaking, I will direct you to that book for further reading.

Internet of Things, Smart Devices

From about 2015 onward, building an internet connection into pretty much every kind of device and home appliance became the new normal. Thermostats to cars to coffee makers to refrigerators to toilets were suddenly collecting data and transmitting it to the cloud. I'm not sure anyone made a truly compelling argument about why toilets had to collect data, but perhaps if you are trying to measure and optimize water usage, it could make sense.

That's the critical point, though: When it's this easy to make devices "smart" and "connected," how do you make sure you're designing IoT and smart device experiences to be meaningful, and in line with the Tech Humanist approach?

Does the data and connectivity end up being used in a way to solve a meaningful problem?

Adding data tracking to a coffee maker because it taps into a market trend for smart appliances is most likely going to cause the company and the consumer more headaches than it's worth in the long run. Ideally, the sensors, data tracking, or connectivity will be shown to solve some kind of problem that has plagued both the company and the consumer. Making the coffee maker just smart enough, say, to sense when buildup inside the machine needs cleaning out? Well, that's another story. A feature like that would extend the maker's life and preserve the flavor of the coffee.

Is the data it collects going to be safeguarded? It's pointless to add data tracking that doesn't meaningfully solve a problem, especially if the additional data collected by the company is going to add risk of breach.

Here again, a sense of purpose, of alignment, and of focusing on meaningful experiences goes a long way.

The Automated Future

It's easy to think of automation as a far-off future idea, when in reality we've been surrounded by automation for decades. Mechanical automation of various sorts has been around for centuries, and large-scale industrial robots have been part of modern manufacturing since at least the 1980s. Automated Teller Machines, or ATMs (note: *not* "ATM machines," since that would be equivalent to saying "Automated Teller Machine machines") became ubiquitous in the last decades of the twentieth century. By now, the idea of interacting with a machine to withdraw cash is routine. Self-checkout lanes at grocery stores and other retailers have also become increasingly common in the last few decades.

Some people resist these forms of replacement of human interaction and human work, but there is no doubt they've become a part of our landscape.

Autonomous Cars

When self-driving cars truly find their way into the mainstream, we will see massive impact of automation.

It offers a form of freedom, and a trap. We make this tradeoff with a lot of technology, but it is particularly notable in this example since the term itself provokes this reflection.

It's interesting to think about what "autonomy" means in the context of autonomous cars. The cars are driven by encoded logic, which operates autonomously and requires no or little interaction from the passengers. But the passenger, who would otherwise be a driver, could also be said to be experiencing a form of autonomy. There's a relinquishing of control, but with that comes the ability to use the ride duration for activities like reading, playing games, watching entertainment, and so on.

From a business logistics standpoint and a service to human needs, there is also the use case of fleets in delivery services, and automating those last-mile logistics for retail and other fulfillment needs.

Robotic Process Automation

"The first rule of any technology used in a business is that automation applied to an efficient operation will magnify the efficiency. The second is that automation applied to an inefficient operation will magnify the inefficiency."
— Bill Gates

When people think about automation wiping out jobs, very likely what they're actually imagining (but may not know the term for) is Robotic Process Automation (RPA), or Robotic Business Process Automation (RBPA).

In many cases RPA is being used to garner efficiencies and reduce errors in production, especially with repetitive, rules-based tasks. RPA has relevance to virtually every industry and every discipline, from traditionally back-office functions to front-office. Deploying automation also means a greater opportunity for workflow data capture, so companies can track processes for better accountability and can optimize timing and effort for maximum output. In many cases, the early opportunities for RPA deployment have been where companies had previously invested in offshore outsourcing, such as fielding a portion of customer support requests that followed predictable patterns.

In effect, RPA is the tech-enabled sibling of Business Process Optimization (BPO). The challenge is to resist the temptation to automate meaningless or, as in Bill Gates's famous quote about automation, inefficient processes. Many people have taken issue with the second part of his quote, suggesting that even if a process is inefficient, automation still makes it more efficient. But it's also critically important to examine *why* a process is inefficient, and if some nuanced decision-making is lurking in it somewhere. Automation and nuanced decision-making don't play well together without some kind of human intervention, so even if the inefficient process, once automated, becomes more efficient, it will likely become more meaningless.

The more complex and nuanced the work, the more challenging it is to deploy RPA for it; but as AI capabilities become more sophisticated, the scope of tasks that automation can address will broaden. Which is why, at this point, this process is mostly addressing the types of work people mean when they talk about automating menial or meaningless tasks to free humans up for higher-level thinking and higher-value work. It's also why I repeatedly talk about making sure people are prepared for higher-level work that involves complex judgment calls, nuanced decision-making, and an understanding of context. The question is not whether jobs will be replaced; it is whether we are adequately developing a human-centric transformation strategy, which includes anticipating which jobs will be replaced and training people to take on work that's more qualified for humans than machines.

There's nothing inherently frightening or threatening about RPA as it relates to human potential or human experience if we approach it the Tech Humanist way; in fact, we should be looking at RPA as much as possible to enhance human potential.

Payments

Over the past few years, I've had the experience several times of going out to run errands and forgetting my wallet but not realizing it until I got back home because all my stops supported payment through my phone.

Mobile payments are not automation in the form of robots, but they are part of a set of technologies that represent deepening digitization and automation of constructs we know in the "real" world, like money.

Whether we're paying with a proprietary app with integrated payment methods or the payment built into the phone or wearable's operating system, a significant portion of our transactions already support mobile payment, and a future where it's truly ubiquitous is easy to imagine. The increasing reach is easy to recognize: By early 2018, Google Pay had been installed more than one hundred million times[117], while Apple Pay is expected to reach two hundred million users by 2020[118].

These payment methods are also able to offer privacy and security to the person using them, while collecting data that can illuminate societal buying patterns at scale.

Of course virtual currencies such as Bitcoin are also part of this discussion, but we'll get into that separately in the next section.

Blockchain, Distributed Ledgers, Cryptocurrency

Well beyond Bitcoin, its most familiar use case, the opportunities for blockchain are broad and intriguing. Of course cryptocurrency alone is an intriguing use case, but distributed ledger implementations stand to remake elections, authenticate royalty distributions in entertainment, broker smart contracts, and consolidate individuals' data sharing, to name just a few ways the technology is already being applied and will certainly be further explored. Some people believe that blockchains can lead to a more globally connected, more fairly distributed, more equal world.

Decentralization is one of the key features of blockchain, and is the reason that its promise is both trust and the lack of need for trust. (Both/and.) Its main drawback is its heavy resource consumption due to the server load necessary to update all the ledgers consistently for each transaction. Bitcoin alone has been estimated to consume as much electricity as the country of Nigeria, but advocates say that new approaches to establishing consensus across all copies of the distributed ledger will improve that.[119]

The Tech Humanist approach here would be to look for ways to safeguard information, to distribute ownership, to validate something's authenticity, to track something's movement through a supply chain, and so on—in the name of transparency, privacy, and shared control.

The Immersive Future

If I asked you to picture the technological future if you have no reason to fear it, and to imagine what characterizes it, to visualize clearly how you move around and interact within it, it's very likely that you picture seamless integrations between technologies, a whole set of tools and benefits that exist beyond screens, beyond the limitations of two-dimensional presentation, with interactions that are triggered by your context or some kind of intuitive cue rather than explicit commands. Your data would probably be being passed from one system to another safely and as appropriate to the task so you can just do what you need to do whenever you need to do it. The immersive version of the future has incredible potential to improve the quality of our lives.

That is, if we aren't worried about our jobs being replaced by robots, about invasive data tracking, about government overreach with technology in our lives, about corporations being greedy with our data and manipulating us, about discrimination based on the data collected about us, or about providing for our financial, medical, and social needs. If we're not worried about any of that.

So we have to address the systemic issues that support this future with human-centric practices and policies. Because the Tech Humanist potential for immersive experiences is too exciting to stifle with thinking that's too small, too selfish, or too short-term.

Platforms, Extensible Frameworks, API Thinking

❋ ❋ ❋

Early in my career in technology, I was responsible for writing documentation for APIs (application programming interfaces) and for compiling SDKs (software development kits). When I first started to do the work, I looked around for inspiration and found it surprising and disappointing that most of the existing examples of this sort of documentation that I could find were so devoid of any insight into how humans might actually use the resulting code integration. In other words, code-level objects and protocols were described as if they existed in a vacuum, or at least only within the context of the rest of the code. Few examples I found showed use cases, meaningful sample code, or anything that would provide software developers with any kind of empathetic connection to the work they were doing.

That was in the 1990s, and APIs are still an important construct in software and technology design. Extensible software and frameworks have "hooks" that can integrate with other software and frameworks, so one set of tools can "call" another set of tools and provide more-than-the-sum-of-its-parts value to the end user. Today, software powering the technology from smartphones to cars to banks to healthcare providers to Twitter to Expedia provides this kind of extensibility, and the opportunity to build one application from another application.

The overall API model is useful as a metaphor, too, in thinking about business opportunities integrating with each other for the benefit of the people who use them. If integrating another service or product somehow into our product, our platform, our service, or our framework makes it both easier for the end user and more successful for us, then we should be proactively developing strategy that fosters those kinds of connections.

The Tech Humanist future is immersive because it leans so heavily on and benefits so much from integration. What stands to make the experiences of the Tech Humanist future more meaningful is the opportunity to learn from the shortcomings of previous generations of software and to use empathy to anticipate human needs, bringing disparate points of information together to dimensionalize decision-making and solve human problems while scalably fulfilling a business objective.

I should note here that APIs themselves deserve good design, too; after all it is humans who are doing the code to integrate, so their experience matters as well. And they will understand better how to make the experience better for the end users if they can empathize with how the integration will solve human problems.

We can't afford to write software developers and other technologists off as uninterested in their fellow humans. First of all, with the majority of the thousands and thousands of technologists I have known in my twenty-year career in technology, that is simply not true; and second, the Tech Humanist approach demands that we expect human values in technology as it scales around us.

Mixed Reality for Storytelling and Empathy

As we look for ways not only for humans to make better technology but also for technology to make us better humans, one of the fields that has long held a great deal of promise has been mixed reality (meaning either augmented reality or virtual reality, or some combination of both). Advocates have promoted it for storytelling because of its believed ability to foster empathy.

A branch of technology research that seeks to deepen people's understanding of one another, Empathic Computing, focuses heavily on mixed reality as one of the most powerful and promising technologies for the purpose because a user can share the gaze of another person (or participate in a body ownership illusion[120], as some researchers describe the experience) as they navigate real-time interactions and decisions that help create a narrative of what it's like to live as that person. In practice, people experience limitations of empathy for a range of reasons, from their existing biases, to the fatigue of using the devices like VR headsets that the experiences rely on.

But there are still exciting examples emerging all the time. During the summer of 2018 when a team of young soccer players was trapped in a cave in Thailand, one of the major media outlets launched an AR-assisted story experience to help readers understand the complexities associated with the rescue. The story used visual layers to illustrate the path through the cave and the tight passages rescuers had to lead the boys through. Importantly, the story display experience was also cleverly designed to be responsive to its container so that it offered a version suitable for older browsers and devices that still provided insight.

So there's work to do on reaching the full potential of MR to achieve understanding between people, and to use it to help us become the best humans we can. It's also not going to work really well until the people creating mixed reality experiences represent a broad cross section of humanity and can tell a diverse range of stories through the medium.

Provide Focus on Relevant Experience

While being surrounded with immersive technologies that creative additive capabilities is exciting, it's also easy to imagine the need for reductive experiences: tools that help us streamline the information around us and focus on what's important.

In some contexts, AR could be a focusing experience. If you can clear away clutter and extraneous information for someone and provide them with additional context and dimension about a selected element, you may help them make decisions more efficiently and with less anxiety.

A simple example of this is the Blippar app, which provides additional keywords and concepts related to whatever is in focus. If I want to explore and better understand something in my surroundings, a tool that lets me choose the conceptual direction for my next steps is a boon.

Other examples are distraction-free writing interfaces (I'm using one now as I write this), noise-cancelling headphones (also using these), and ad blocker extensions for browsers. The possibilities for alignment here are wide-reaching. What tool can you offer to people who use your product or service that helps them stay focused on their objectives and that fulfills your business goals?

The Intelligent Future

❀ ❀ ❀

Sometimes the things that excite us the most are also the most frightening. That certainly seems to be the case with artificial intelligence, judging from the nonstop discussion of it in business, in the media, and in popular culture. Most people can readily imagine why AI could be transformative to human existence in thrilling ways, enabling us to achieve more than ever before. But most people can also readily imagine disastrous dystopian outcomes. What people seem to fear when they think about AI run amok is the "Singularity," or what theoretically happens when Generalized Artificial Intelligence becomes sentient and self-aware; when AI gains consciousness, free will, and a destructive or even merely disinterested attitude toward humanity.

People often get confused about the difference between algorithms, automation, and artificial intelligence, as well as the abundance of more specific terms within these areas, such as machine learning, cognitive computing, deep learning, and so on, which only adds to the confusion and anxiety around the space. So in this section, I will offer a brief overview on terminology, and some of the key differences in thinking about aligning business objectives and human objectives.

We've already discussed automation and the field of Robotic Process Automation. We'll unpack a few additional terms and concepts around AI to try to help make sense of what's what and what's next.

Machine Learning, Deep Learning, Conversational AI, Natural Language Processing

You practically need artificial intelligence to keep track of the terms that describe the various kinds of artificial intelligence. Rather than write a book within a book about it, in this section I'll briefly cover two of the terms for how machines gather and process their information, and two of the terms that refer to how the information can be applied in practice.

Within the technologies that AI describes, people often refer to machine learning and deep learning. It can be helpful to understand the differences between the terms and ideas behind them.

Machine learning uses algorithms to sift through data and parse it for patterns.

Deep learning is a form of machine learning that uses an Artificial Neural Network to learn on its own and self-correct. Google AlphaGo is an example of deep learning in application. Deep learning is, in a sense, the most humanlike of artificial intelligence capabilities, since it can learn on its own.

Some of the most meaningful interactive human experiences are a lot like a conversation, so when it comes to applying these types of machine learning to human experiences, very often Conversational AI and Natural Language Processing come into play.

For example, Conversational AI that adapts to the interaction may be really useful if your offering has to do with task-based interactive capabilities, such as:

- Booking travel, restaurants, or resources
- Healthcare updates
- Finance and accounting, such as the popular app Trim that monitors patterns in your spending and alerts you when you're spending more than usual or when you have an opportunity to eliminate a recurring charge

Natural Language Processing, or Natural Language Understanding, is a computing approach that attempts to have computers handle requests and interactions in human languages as they're spoken and written.

But NLP is concerned with free text as a person might ask a question or issue an instruction, whereas Conversational AI could be about creating a conversation-like experience that may use text, commands, audio, or images. It may include NLP if free text parsing is involved.

The difference between Natural Language Processing and Conversational AI can be confusing. They're certainly not mutually exclusive. They can be used together effectively.

AI and the Future of Humanity

AI is not a far-off fiction; the research and work around AI have powered smartphones and virtual assistants as we know them now.

As for the artificially intelligent experiences of the future, one school of thought is extremely cautionary about the machine-dominated dystopia we may be creating; another is optimistically exuberant about a highly evolved post-work, post-discrimination utopia.

You can find experts who fall anywhere along those prediction extremes, but the "both/and" integrated pragmatic takeaway of the Tech Humanist approach is this: We are encoding the machines ourselves. We develop the data models, we determine the initial rules by which algorithms decide important content and experiences for us. And today's algorithms are tomorrow's AI.

Business will see tremendous, unprecedented gains from the efficiencies of intelligent automation. The next generation of business stands to either accelerate so much that it tears itself further away from serving the needs of humanity, or evolve to align itself more closely with human objectives and outcomes for the good of us all.

In the meantime, the reality is: AI isn't always as good as most people think. And humans? Pretty often, we're better than most of us think.

Don't get me wrong: I've seen a lot of demonstrations of AI that made my jaw drop. But I also regularly hear from many of the people building it that, fundamentally, AI still struggles with a lot of the same challenges it faced twenty years ago, just on faster hardware.

Meanwhile, humans are the ones who have built AI thus far, and we're the ones laying the groundwork for what's to come. The best thing we can do is work on our own evolution to make sure *we're* as good as we need to be while we're encoding machines that will shape so much of our future experiences.

What will serve us best is to remain humble about our abilities and imbue the technology we create with as much consideration for human dignity in as many ways as possible. That means working toward mediating bias in big data and algorithms and infusing empathetic nuance and context into automated experiences.

With increasingly adaptive cognitive computing, we have significant cognitive power to assist human capabilities and solve many of humanity's greatest challenges.

We have the power to make the future as positive and promising for all of humanity as we decide to do.

If your business stands to benefit from AI, and most businesses probably do, it is imperative for your business as well as for humanity to develop human-centric data models and strategies, and to evaluate the implications of your work at scale for culture, for human connection, for human prosperity, and for human potential. I genuinely cannot emphasize that enough.

CHAPTER 33

EPILOGUE: The Integrated Future

NOW THAT YOU'VE READ THIS book, the decision is yours: How will you bring these ideas to life in your work? Will you join the ranks of the Tech Humanists, actively working toward a world where business objectives and technological progress can align with and enhance human objectives?

How will we make sure we are creating the most meaningful human experiences while adapting our businesses to the future?

How can we embrace the best of what business offers while honoring the truth of humanity?

Let Our Humanity Lead Us

No matter how rapidly technology changes our interactions and our surroundings, what remains the same is our human nature. We all have senses, awareness, and intelligence, and we can all make meaning from what happens around us. We can let our humanity lead us. It can lead us by demonstrating what we have in common, by grounding our work in technology in the human scale, and by helping us appreciate the humanity of others. We can use technology to create more accessible, useful, meaningful experiences for other humans that succeed wildly in business terms. We can demonstrate a baseline level of common respect for which we can respect ourselves. I HAVE READ THIS

Stay Grounded

Part of our shared human experience is in relation to the earth we live on. We know what it's like to stand or sit on solid ground, which is to say we know the human experience of gravity. We know what it's like to breathe fresh air, which is to say we know the human experience of atmosphere. If someday we expand our footprint to other planets in a significant way, these common reference points may change; and the shared understanding of gravity, atmosphere, geography, common landscapes, and so on will be gone. Our relationship to our planet, to physical space, to existence on earth is one of our most baseline common experiences, and easily overlooked. To keep experiences meaningful, they must maintain a connection to our physical experiences. I believe we can't give these up completely. Virtual reality experiences may be alternatives that entertain, educate, and serve a variety of other functions, but they are not replacements. We need a functioning earth, which means we need business models that allow for a sustainable relationship to the resources they consume, and when possible, human experiences that enrich our awareness of our surroundings and deepen our connection to the earth.

Stay in Touch with Our Senses

Our senses help us make meaning. We take in all sorts of data through our senses. So no matter what changes, to stay close to our ability to create and appreciate meaning, we as humans need to stay in touch with our senses. When in doubt about the experiences you create, come back to the senses.

Not only do experiences that offer sensory appeal keep us grounded in our humanity, but also they enrich the connection between brand and customer. Interfaces and interactions that accomplish the task while offering, say, a pleasing touch interface, a visually rich environment, a pleasant notification sound, or, in a physical environment, an aroma that conjures up metaphors that dimensionalize the value of the exchange can make the experience more memorable and more meaningful. It's a win for business and a win for humanity.

Owning Our Attention and Awareness

Given that most of us are already carrying always-on devices that connect us to the largest repository of human knowledge and interaction the world has ever seen, much of which is delivered in a way that is designed to be addictive, it's easy to understand why we find ourselves distracted from our most pressing tasks and from our immediate physical surroundings. And as our experiences more and more rely on smart speakers and earbuds that listen for commands, goggles and glasses that intercept our vision, smart jewelry and accessories that provide haptic and visual notifications, massive screens in public spaces, and so on, we will find it easier and easier to have our attention pulled to some kind of technological trigger.

But there will continue to be value in being intentional about where our attention goes, and in being mindful and present with the people we want to share a connection with.

Human to Human / "Human-Scale" (Like in Architecture)

Building an operation around automation and AI ensures its potential to grow massively, to accelerate beyond human speed, to conduct interactions with virtually no limits, and to generate and concentrate enormous wealth and power. These are intriguing capabilities, but they pack some risks: the risk of making human-powered operations irrelevant, the risk of delivering individual human experiences erroneously and potentially at great harm, and the risk of overshadowing the appeal of the human scale. Although humans prefer avoiding other humans at times, we also thrive on interacting with each other, building communities together, supporting each other, and feeling a sense of connection with each other.

Architects talk about "human scale" structures, in which even a five-hundred-foot-high building might have elements that relate to the way humans interact with it, such as overhangs that emphasize the entrance and accentuate its appropriate form to a human's size. It's an important concept to borrow as we develop machine-driven experiences. We will do well to consider the value of the human scale in building digital environments and interactions.

Remember Purpose

And remember: You can always come back to purpose, which is the shape meaning takes in business.

When all else fails and you don't know what the next step needs to be, review your company's purpose. Heck, review your own purpose. And resolve to drive decisions in alignment with it.

The clarity that comes from purpose can illuminate your priorities, simplify your decision-making, streamline your investments, and help you and all the people who are working with you achieve meaningful outcomes. Which is what we need if we're going to have meaningful experiences at scale.

Innovation and What's Next

* * *

We can't stop following the emergence of new technologies and innovations.

It's not slowing down anytime soon anyway. Business drivers will ensure that. How much good comes from it is up to us: If we are willing to do the work of integrating the goals and outcomes, we can truly change the future.

The more of us Tech Humanists there are, the more we can create the best futures for the most people.

Kate O'Neill, the original "Tech Humanist," helps business profitably create better experiences for humans in a future increasingly driven by data and technology. A world-renowned expert in integrated experience strategy, she is the author of several previous books including *Pixels and Place: Connecting Human Experience Across Physical and Digital Spaces*; a frequent keynote speaker presenting to thousands of the world's top executives each year; and founder of KO Insights, an advisory firm offering guidance on innovation, strategy, and digital transformation with clients among the Fortune 500 and beyond. Kate's prior professional roles included first-of-its-kind work at Netflix, Toshiba America, her own digital strategy and analytics firm [meta]marketer, and a variety of digital content and technology start-ups.

Kate has been featured in CNN Money, *TIME*, *Forbes*, *USA Today*, BBC News, and other international media, and has been named "Technology Entrepreneur of the Year," "Power Leader in Technology," and numerous other awards and recognitions. She writes regularly for a variety of publications and is a keen observer of meaningful experiences in business and beyond.

More information about Kate, including ways to connect, can be found at: http://www.koinsights.com/about/about-kate-oneill/

[1] "Chapman University Survey of American Fears 2017," Earl Babbie Research Center, Chapman University, accessed September 13, 2018,

https://www.chapman.edu/wilkinson/research-centers/babbie-center/_files/Chapman-University-fears-by-percentage.pdf.

[2] Stephen G. Hasty Jr., "The next 3 years: CEOs believe it's now or never," *KPMG*, last modified June 27, 2016, https://home.kpmg.com/xx/en/home/insights/2016/06/the-next-3-years-ceos-believe-its-now-or-never.html.

[3] Arthur C. Clarke, "Hazards of Prophecy: The Failure of Imagination," *Profiles of the Future: An Inquiry into the Limits of the Possible* (New York: Harper & Row, 1973).

[4] Dan Amira, "Robot Apocalypse Draws Nearer with IBM's *Jeopardy!* Victory," *New York Magazine*, last modified January 13, 2011, http://nymag.com/daily/intelligencer/2011/01/robot_apocalypse_draws_nearer.html.

[5] "$930 Million," *Quartz*, last modified June 15, 2017, https://index.qz.com/1006412/crowdfunding-health-services-almost-half-of-the-money-raised-through-gofundme-went-to-medical-campaigns.

[6] Paige Kutilek, "Spotlight Statistics About Medical Debt You Need to Know," *GoFundMe*, last modified June 23, 2016, https://www.gofundme.com/c/blog/medical-debt.

[7] Anonymous, "John Henry," *Poetry Foundation*, accessed September 14, 2018, https://www.poetryfoundation.org/poems/42897/john-henry.

[8] Stephen Jay Gould, "Wide hats and narrow minds," Natural History 88, no. 2 (February 1979): 40.

[9] Carl Benedikt Frey and Michael A. Osborne, "The Future of Employment: How Susceptible Are Jobs to Computerisation?" Oxford Martin School, September 17, 2013, https://www.oxfordmartin.ox.ac.uk/downloads/academic/future-of-employment.pdf.

[10] Carl Benedikt Frey and Chinchih Chen, "Technology at Work v3.0: Automating e-Commerce from Click to Pick to Door," Oxford

Martin School, August 2017, https://www.oxfordmartin.ox.ac.uk/publications/view/2581.

[11] Ljubica Nedelkoska and Glenda Quintini, "Automation, skills use and training," OECD, no. 202 (March 8, 2018), https://www.oecd-ilibrary.org/employment/automation-skills-use-and-training_2e2f4eea-en.

[12] Ina Fried, "AI is the future of discrimination—and fairness," *Axios*, last updated August 1, 2018, https://www.axios.com/ai-as-the-future-of-discrimination-fairness-415a69aa-3bf7-476b-88fd-cb95698a6001.html

[13] Rachel Kaser, "AI-powered robot can spot Waldo in 4.5 seconds," *The Next Web*, last modified August 10, 2018, https://thenextweb.com/artificial-intelligence/2018/08/10/ai-powered-robot-can-spot-waldo-in-4-5-seconds.

[14] Rachael Stephens, "Automate This: Building the Perfect 21st-Century Worker," *Third Way*, last modified April 7, 2017, https://www.thirdway.org/report/automate-this-building-the-perfect-21st-century-worker.

[15] The Disney Institute, Be Our Guest: Perfecting the Art of Customer Service, revised edition (New York: Disney Editions, 2001), 19–20.

[16] Neal Ungerleider, "Southwest Airlines' Digital Transformation Takes Off," *Fast Company*, last modified March 27, 2017,

https://www.fastcompany.com/3065045/southwest-airlines-digital-transformation-takes-off.

[17] An archive of the prior version of the Netflix culture deck that became a viral phenomenon is at Reed Hastings's SlideShare: https://www.slideshare.net/reed2001/culture-1798664; and a current Netflix culture statement lives on the company website at: https://jobs.netflix.com/culture.

[18] Patty McCord, "How Netflix Reinvented HR," *Harvard Business Review* (January–February 2014), https://hbr.org/2014/01/how-netflix-reinvented-hr.

[19] "Open Letter to the Airbnb Community About Building a 21st Century Company," *Airbnb Press Room*, last modified January 25, 2018, https://press.atairbnb.com/brian-cheskys-open-letter-to-the-airbnb-community-about-building-a-21st-century-company.

[20] Michael Chui, James Manyika, Mehdi Miremadi, "Four fundamentals of workplace automation," *McKinsey Quarterly* (November 2015), https://www.mckinsey.com/business-functions/digital-mckinsey/our-insights/four-fundamentals-of-workplace-automation.

[21] F. Scott Fitzgerald, "The Crack-Up," *Esquire*, last modified March 7, 2017, https://www.esquire.com/lifestyle/a4310/the-crack-up. Originally published in 1936.

[22] Caleb Gayle, "US gig economy: data shows 16m people in 'contingent or alternative' work," *Guardian*, last modified June 7, 2018, https://www.theguardian.com/business/2018/jun/07/america-gig-economy-work-bureau-labor-statistics.

[23] Julia Shults, "Nashville Fashion Alliance: Growing an Industry from Scratch," *StyleBlueprint*, last accessed September 15, 2018, https://styleblueprint.com/nashville/everyday/nashville-fashion-alliance.

[24] Full disclosure: I served on the executive board of the Nashville Fashion Alliance from 2014, just prior to its formal founding in 2015, through 2016. But I cannot take a bit of credit for the brilliance of the sewing academy program.

[25] Matt Laukaitis, "Technology Is Rewriting The Rules Of Retail," Digitalist Mag, last modified May 1, 2018, https://www.digitalistmag.com/customer-experience/2018/05/01/technology-is-rewriting-rules-of-retail-06136740.

[26] Lydia Dishman, "Why The Hiring Process Takes Longer Than Ever," *Fast Company*, last modified July 13, 2015, https://www.fastcompany.com/3048421/why-the-hiring-process-takes-longer-than-ever.

[27] Sylvia Ann Hewlett, Melinda Marshall, and Laura Sherbin, "How Diversity Can Drive Innovation," *Harvard Business Review* (December 2013), https://hbr.org/2013/12/how-diversity-can-drive-innovation.

[28] American Sociological Association, "Research links diversity with increased sales revenue and profits, more customers," *EurekAlert*, last modified March 31, 2009, https://www.eurekalert.org/pub_releases/2009-03/asa-rld033009.php.

[29] "The Internet of Trains," Teradata, last accessed September 15,

2018, http://assets.teradata.com/resourceCenter/downloads/CaseStudies/EB8903.pdf.

[30] "Supply Chain Disclosure," *Rebecca Minkoff*, last accessed September 15, 2018, https://www.rebeccaminkoff.com/pages/supply-chain-disclosure.

[31] Steve O'Hear, "Karma raises $12M to let restaurants and grocery stores offer unsold food at a discount," *TechCrunch*, last accessed September 15, 2018, https://techcrunch.com/2018/08/15/karma-life.

[32] Catherine Shu, "Shelf Engine uses machine learning to stop food waste from eating into store margins," *TechCrunch*, last accessed September 15, 2018, https://techcrunch.com/2018/08/15/shelf-engine-uses-machine-learning-to-stop-food-waste-from-eating-into-store-margins.

[33] Danny Crichton, "Fighting food waste, Full Harvest raises $8.5m to bring excess produce to commercial buyers," *TechCrunch*, last accessed September 15, 2018, https://techcrunch.com/2018/08/15/full-harvest-series-a.

[34] Steve O'Hear, "Digi.me and Personal merge to put you in control of the nascent 'personal data ecosystem,'" *TechCrunch*, last modified August 17, 2017, https://techcrunch.com/2017/08/17/digi-me-and-personal-merge/.

[35] Louis Columbus, "10 Charts That Will Change Your Perspective of Amazon Prime's Growth," *Forbes*, last modified March 4, 2018, https://www.forbes.com/sites/louiscolumbus/2018/03/04/10-charts-that-will-change-your-perspective-of-amazon-primes-growth/#4ad33023feea.

[36] Ingrid Lunden, "Amazon's share of the US e-commerce market is now 49%, or 5% of all retail spend," *TechCrunch*, last accessed September 15, 2018, https://techcrunch.com/2018/07/13/amazons-share-of-the-us-e-commerce-market-is-now-49-or-5-of-all-retail-spend.

[37] Hindi Kornbluth (@Hindividual), "Yay!! This makes me so happy ! @raemadeline and I are engineers at RTR and we made this as a hack week project earlier this year because we really wanted the feature, and it's so awesome to see other people enjoying it!" Twitter, June 27, 2018, 10:57 a.m., https://twitter.com/Hindividual/status/1012001889943195648

[38] Kathryn Vasel, "JetBlue just made WiFi free on all domestic flights," *CNN Money*, last modified January 11, 2017, https://money.cnn.com/2017/01/11/pf/jetblue-free-wiffi-all-domestic-flights.

[39] Alex Samuely, "JetBlue flies in Apple Pay for in-flight purchases, seating upgrades," *RetailDive*, last accessed September 15, 2018, https://www.retaildive.com/ex/mobilecommercedaily/jetblue-flies-in-apple-pay-to-enable-easy-purchases-of-snacks-premium-seating.

[40] Ruben Green, "Three Great Tree-Identification Apps for Your Smart Phone," *Evergreen Arborist Consultants*, last modified January 16, 2017, https://greenarborists.com/three-great-tree-identification-apps-smart-phone.

[41] Nick Douglas, "Shazam for Birds: Three Apps That Recognize Bird Calls," *Lifehacker*, last modified September 18, 2017, https://lifehacker.com/shazam-for-birds-three-apps-that-recognize-bird-calls-1797955537.

[42] "NASA Nanotechnology-Based Biosensor Helps Detect Biohazards," *NASA.gov*, last modified May 20, 2008, https://www.nasa.gov/centers/ames/news/releases/2008/08_45AR.html.

[43] Clare McGrane, "Mindshare Medical launches AI cancer screening tech that can see 'data beyond our reception,'" *Geekwire*, last modified August 2, 2018, https://www.geekwire.com/2018/mindshare-medical-launches-ai-cancer-screening-tech-can-see-data-beyond-perception.

[44] Fu-Chen Chen and Mohammad R. Jahanshahi, "NB-CNN: Deep Leaning-Based Crack Detection Using Convolutional Neural Network and Naïve Bayes Data Fusion," *IEEE Transactions on Industrial Electronics* 65, no. 5 (May 2018): https://ieeexplore.ieee.org/document/8074762.

[45] Péralte C. Paul, "ATDC Startup Paretic Acquired," *ATDC Georgia Tech*, last modified November 2, 2016, http://atdc.org/atdc-news/atdc-startup-partpic-acquired.

[46] "Summary of Hours of Service Regulations," *Federal Motor Carrier Safety Administration*, last modified March 9, 2017, https://www.fmcsa.dot.gov/regulations/hours-service/summary-hours-service-regulations.

[47] Michael H. Belzer, *Sweatshops on Wheels: Winners and Losers in*

Trucking Deregulation (Oxford: Oxford University Press, 2000).

[48] Bureau of Labor Statistics, "Occupational Outlook Handbook: Heavy and Tractor-trailer Truck Drivers," *US Department of Labor*, last modified April 13, 2018, https://www.bls.gov/ooh/transportation-and-material-moving/heavy-and-tractor-trailer-truck-drivers.htm.

[49] "Proudly Brewed. Self-Driven," *Otto*, last modified October 25, 2016, https://blog.ot.to/proudly-brewed-self-driven-95268c520ba4.

[50] Romain Dillet, "Uber acquires Otto to lead Uber's self-driving car effort," *TechCrunch*, last modified August 18, 2016, https://techcrunch.com/2016/08/18/uber-acquires-otto-to-lead-ubers-self-driving-car-effort-report-says.

[51] Jillian D'Onfro, "Uber's purchase of Otto looks like it was much cheaper than originally reported," *CNBC*, last modified December 14, 2017, https://www.cnbc.com/2017/12/14/ieee-analysis-shows-uber-paid-as-little-as-220-million-for-otto.html.

[52] "Mcity Test Facility," *UMich.edu*, last accessed September 15, 2018, https://mcity.umich.edu/our-work/mcity-test-facility.

[53] https://www.npr.org/2018/08/07/636347531/hundreds-of-bikes-dumped-at-dallas-recycling-center-as-ofo-leaves-market

[54] "Worldwide Wearables Market to Nearly Double by 2021, According to IDC," *International Data Corporation*, last modified June 21, 2017, https://www.idc.com/getdoc.jsp?containerId=prUS42818517.

[55] Sam Barker, "Future Digital Advertising: AI, Ad Fraud & Ad Blocking 2017-2022," *Juniper Research*, last modified September 25, 2017, https://www.juniperresearch.com/researchstore/content-commerce/future-digital-advertising/ai-ad-fraud-ad-blocking-2017-2022.

[56] Joe Rossignol, "Apple Says AirPods Are 'Incredibly Popular' as Availability Remains Limited," *MacRumors*, last modified May 2, 2018, https://www.macrumors.com/2018/05/02/apple-says-airpods-incredibly-popular.

[57] Michael Sawh, "Project Jacquard guide: The lowdown on Google and Levi's smart jacket," *Wareable*, last modified September 25, 2017, https://www.wareable.com/smart-clothing/google-levis-project-jacquard-release-date-2750.

[58] "Wearable Medical Devices Market by Device (Diagnostic (Heart, Pulse, BP, Sleep), Therapeutic (Pain, Insulin, Rehabilitation), Application (Sport, Fitness, RPM), Type (Smartwatch, Patch), Distribution Channel (Pharmacy, Online) - Global Forecast to 2022," *MarketsandMarkets*, last modified January 2018, https://www.marketsandmarkets.com/Market-Reports/wearable-medical-device-market-81753973.html.

[59] Henry Anhalt, "Applying Digital Technology in Clinical Trials to Improve Real-World Outcomes," *American Journal of Managed Care*, last modified March 31, 2018, https://www.ajmc.com/journals/evidence-based-diabetes-management/2018/march-2018/applying-digital-technology-in-clinical-trials-to-improve-real-world-outcomes.

[60] Rebecca Hills-Duty, "Lemnis Technologies Announce Platform For Reducing Simulation Sickness," VRFocus, last modified August 15, 2018, https://www.vrfocus.com/2018/08/lemnis-technologies-announce-platform-for-reducing-simulation-sickness.

[61] Kevin Coldewey, "VR optics could help old folks keep the world in focus," *TechCrunch*, last modified August 15, 2018, https://techcrunch.com/2018/08/15/vr-optics-could-help-old-folks-keep-the-world-in-focus.

[62] Rob Thubron, "Smart Speaker installs expected to hit 100 million this year, but HomePods make up just 4% of market," *TechSpot*, last modified July 10, 2018, https://www.techspot.com/news/75427-smart-speaker-installs-expected-hit-100-million-year.html.

[63] Ashley Halsey III, "Study: Voice-activated texting while driving no safer than typing," *The Washington Post*, April 23, 2013. https://www.washingtonpost.com/local/trafficandcommuting/study-voice-activated-texting-while-driving-no-safer-than-typing/2013/04/22/e0ec6780-a859-11e2-8302-3c7e0ea97057_story.html

[64] M.A. Regan and E. Mitsopoulos, "Understanding Passenger Influences on Driver Behaviour: Implications for Road Safety and Recommendations for Countermeasure Development," *Monash University Accident Research Centre*, last modified April 2001, https://www.monash.edu/muarc/our-publications/muarc180.

[65] Melissa Locker, "Apple's podcasts just topped 50 billion all-time downloads and streams," *Fast Company*, last modified April 25, 2018, https://www.fastcompany.com/40563318/apples-podcasts-just-

topped-50-billion-all-time-downloads-and-streams.

[66] Peter Burrows, "The future is ear: Why 'hearables' are finally tech's next big thing," *Fast Company*, last modified August 2, 2018, https://www.fastcompany.com/90212065/the-future-is-ear-why-hearables-are-finally-techs-next-big-thing.

[67] David Baker, "Identity 2016: Facebook lets blind people 'see' its photos," *BBC*, last modified April 5, 2016, https://www.bbc.com/news/disability-35881779.

[68] "Woebot's friends come from all walks of life," *Woebot*, last accessed September 15, 2018, https://woebot.io/community.

[69] "Meet Wysa," *Wysa*, last accessed September 15, 2018, https://www.wysa.io.

[70] Marshall Allen, "Health Insurers Are Vacuuming Up Details About You—And It Could Raise Your Rates," *ProPublica*, last modified July 17, 2018, https://www.propublica.org/article/health-insurers-are-vacuuming-up-details-about-you-and-it-could-raise-your-rates.

[71] P. Jeffrey Brantingham, Matthew Valasik, and George O. Mohler, "Does Predictive Policing Lead to Biased Arrests? Results From a Randomized Controlled Trial," *Statistics and Public Policy* 5, no. 1 (February 8, 2018):
https://amstat.tandfonline.com/doi/full/10.1080/2330443X.2018.1438940#.W5Q32ZNKjUI.

[72] Will Oremus, "Facebook's Broken Promises," *Slate*, last modified November 24, 2017, http://www.slate.com/articles/technology/technology/2017/11/why_facebook_broke_its_promise_to_stop_allowing_racist_housing_ads.html.

[73] Alana Semuels, "A House You Can Buy, But Never Own," *Atlantic*, last modified April 10, 2018, https://www.theatlantic.com/business/archive/2018/04/rent-to-own-redlining/557588.

[74] Dave Gershgorn, "America's biggest body-camera company says facial recognition isn't accurate enough for policing decisions," *Quartz*, last modified August 8, 2018, https://qz.com/1351519/facial-recognition-isnt-yet-accurate-enough-for-policing-decisions.

[75] Jon Schuppe, "Facial recognition gives police a powerful new tracking tool. It's also raising alarms," *NBC News*, last modified July 30, 2018, https://www.nbcnews.com/news/us-news/facial-recognition-

gives-police-powerful-new-tracking-tool-it-s-n894936.

[76] "Open Platform," *Guardian*, last accessed September 15, 2018, https://open-platform.theguardian.com.

[77] "Atlas Van Lines," *OpenData 500 Global Network*, last accessed September 15, 2018, http://www.opendata500.com/us/atlas-van-lines.

[78] Kate O'Neill, Lessons from Los Gatos: How Working at a Startup Called Netflix Made Me a Better Entrepreneur (and Mentor) (Amazon Digital Services: 2014).

[79] James Collins. *Good to Great: Why Some Companies Make the Leap… and Others Don't* (New York: HarperBusiness, 2001).

[80] Josef Adalian, "Inside the Binge Factory," *Vulture*, last modified June 11, 2018, http://www.vulture.com/2018/06/how-netflix-swallowed-tv-industry.html.

[81] "Dell Technologies Capital," *Crunchbase*, last accessed September 15, 2018, https://www.crunchbase.com/organization/dell-technologies-capital#section-overview.

[82] Joseph L. Bower and Clayton M. Christensen, "Disruptive Technologies: Catching the Wave," *Harvard Business Review*, (January–February 1995), https://hbr.org/1995/01/disruptive-technologies-catching-the-wave.

[83] Alex Moazed and Nicholas Johnson, "Why Clayton Christensen Is Wrong About Uber And Disruptive Innovation," *TechCrunch*, last modified February 27, 2016, https://techcrunch.com/2016/02/27/why-clayton-christensen-is-wrong-about-uber-and-disruptive-innovation.

[84] "Data & Society," *Data & Society Research Institute*, last accessed September 15, 2018, https://datasociety.net.

[85] "AI Now," last accessed September 15, 2018, https://ainowinstitute.org.

[86] "The Trolley Problem: Philosophers Take On The Ethics Of AVs," *Progrss*, last modified February 16, 2018, https://progrss.com/movement/20180216/trolley-problem.

[87] Arlene Weintraub, "Artificial Intelligence Is Infiltrating Medicine—But Is It Ethical?," *Forbes*, last modified March 16, 2018, https://www.forbes.com/sites/arleneweintraub/2018/03/16/artificial-intelligence-is-infiltrating-medicine-but-is-it-ethical/#16067a903a24.

[88] EU GDPR Information Portal, last accessed September 15,

2018, https://www.eugdpr.org.

[89] Nick Wingfield, "Amazon Pushes Facial Recognition to Police. Critics See Surveillance Risk," *The Washington Post*, May 22, 2018. https://www.nytimes.com/2018/05/22/technology/amazon-facial-recognition.html

[90] Will Knight, "The World Economic Forum warns that AI may destabilize the financial system," *MIT Technology Review*, last modified August 15, 2018, https://www.technologyreview.com/s/611890/the-world-economic-forum-warns-that-ai-may-destabilize-the-financial-system.

[91] Samantha Cole, "There Is No Tech Solution to Deepfakes," *VICE*, last modified August 14, 2018, https://motherboard.vice.com/en_us/article/594qx5/there-is-no-tech-solution-to-deepfakes.

[92] University of Bath, "AI could make dodgy lip sync dubbing a thing of the past," *ScienceDaily*, last modified August 17, 2018, https://www.sciencedaily.com/releases/2018/08/180817125402.htm.

[93] Devin Coldewey, "Laying a trap for self-driving cars," *TechCrunch*, last modified March 17, 2017, https://techcrunch.com/2017/03/17/laying-a-trap-for-self-driving-cars.

[94] Yutaka Suzuki, Lisa Galli, Ayaka Ikeda, Shoji Itakura, and Michiteru Kitazaki, "Measuring empathy for human and robot hand pain using electroencephalography," *Nature* 5 (November 3, 2015): https://www.nature.com/articles/srep15924.

[95] Jim Isaak, "The Danger of Empathy for Robots," *Technology and Society*, last modified April 13, 2018, http://technologyandsociety.org/danger-empathy-robots.

[96] Jeff Robbins, "We Are Becoming Enslaved by Our Technology —Ruminations on the IQ2 Debate," *Technology and Society*, last modified June 29, 2017, http://technologyandsociety.org/ruminations-on-the-iq2-debate-we-are-becoming-enslaved-by-our-technology.

[97] Kurt Wagner, "I talked to Google's Duplex voice assistant. It felt like the beginning of something big," *Recode*, last modified June 27, 2018, https://www.recode.net/2018/6/27/17508166/google-duplex-assistant-demo-voice-calling-ai.

[98] "2016 Aspect Consumer Experience Index," *Aspect.com*, last modified October 26, 2016, https://www.aspect.com/globalassets/2016-aspect-consumer-experience-index-survey_index-results-final.pdf.

[99] Omar Oakes, "Consumers sometimes trust chatbots more than other humans, says survey," *Campaign*, last modified June 30, 2016, https://www.campaignlive.co.uk/article/consumers-sometimes-trust-chatbots-humans-says-survey/1400821.

[100] "2016 Aspect Consumer Experience Index," *Aspect.com*, last modified October 26, 2016, https://www.aspect.com/globalassets/2016-aspect-consumer-experience-index-survey_index-results-final.pdf.

[101] Or as my friend Jeffrey Zeldman jokingly abbreviates it: IHED.

[102] Karen Lo, "Chief Daniel Humm on the Influence of Miles Davis, The Stones," The Daily Meal, last modified June 11, 2014, https://www.thedailymeal.com/news/chef-daniel-humm-eleven-madison-park-influence-miles-davis-rolling-stones/61114.

[103] Ryan Sutton, "Eleven Madison Park Names 'World's Best Restaurant,'" Eater, last modified April 5, 2017, https://www.eater.com/2017/4/5/15188712/eleven-madison-park-worlds-best-restaurant-2017.

[104] George E. P. Box, William Hunter and Stuart Hunter, *Statistics for Experimenters*, second edition, 2005, page 440

[105] Stands for "Fear of Missing Out" — the phenomenon of envy at how much more fabulous than yours your digital acquaintances' lives apparently are.

[106] Stands for "too long; didn't read" — often used to preface a brief Twitter-length summary of a longer piece of writing.

[107] Jim Collins, "Hedgehog Concept in the Business Sectors," JimCollins.com, last accessed September 17, 2018, http://www.jimcollins.com/article_topics/articles/hedgehog-concept-business-sectors.html.

[108] Adam Withal, "Uber knows when your phone is running out of battery," *Independent*, last modified May 22, 2016, http://www.independent.co.uk/life-style/gadgets-and-tech/news/uber-knows-when-your-phone-is-about-to-run-out-of-battery-a7042416.html.

[109] Kyle Wiggers, "Google is reportedly developing an AI assistant that recommends workouts and meal plans," *VentureBeat*, last modified August 15, 2018, https://venturebeat.com/2018/08/15/google-is-reportedly-developing-an-ai-assistant-that-recommends-workouts-and-meal-plans.

[110] Chuck Salter, "OXO's Favorite Mistakes," *Fast Company*, last

modified October 1, 2005, https://www.fastcompany.com/54174/oxos-favorite-mistakes.

[111] "Human-Centered Design Prompts for Emerging Technologies," *Google*, last accessed September 17, 2018, http://services.google.com/fh/files/blogs/ideo_design_prompts_emerging_tech.pdf.

[112] Nathan Jensen, "238 cities are wooing Amazon. The winner may end up with a very bad deal," *Washington Post*, last modified October 24, 2017, https://www.washingtonpost.com/news/monkey-cage/wp/2017/10/24/238-cities-are-bidding-to-tempt-amazon-to-build-the-winner-may-end-up-with-a-very-bad-deal/?utm_term=.ea8648c6c5f8.

[113] Amy Liu, "Landing Amazon HQ2 isn't the right way for a city to create jobs. Here's what works instead," *Brookings*, last modified August 7, 2018, https://www.brookings.edu/blog/the-avenue/2018/08/07/landing-amazon-hq2-isnt-the-right-way-for-a-city-to-create-jobs-heres-what-works-instead.

[114] "Sharing City Seoul," *Nesta*, last accessed September 18, 2018, https://www.nesta.org.uk/feature/10-people-centred-smart-city-initiatives/sharing-city-seoul.

[115] "BlockPooling," *Nesta*, last accessed September 18, 2018, https://www.nesta.org.uk/feature/10-people-centred-smart-city-initiatives/blockpooling.

[116] https://www.nesta.org.uk/feature/10-people-centred-smart-city-initiatives/petajakarta/

[117] "Google Pay Now Installed More Than 100 Million Times," *PYMNTS.com*, last modified April 19, 2018, https://www.pymnts.com/news/payment-methods/2018/google-pay-digital-payments-installed-100-million-times.

[118] "Study: Apple Pay to reach 200M users by 2020," last modified June 28, 2018, https://www.mobilepaymentstoday.com/news/study-apple-pay-to-reach-200m-users-by-2020.

[119] Mike Orcutt, "Blockchains Use Massive Amounts of Energy—But There's a Plan to Fix That," *MIT Technology Review*, November 16, 2017. https://www.technologyreview.com/s/609480/bitcoin-uses-massive-amounts-of-energybut-theres-a-plan-to-fix-it/

[120] Philippe Bertrand, Jérôme Guegan, Léonore Robieux, Cade

Andrew McCall, Franck Zenasni, "Learning Empathy Through Virtual Reality: Multiple Strategies for Training Empathy-Related Abilities Using Body Ownership Illusions in Embodied Virtual Reality," *Frontiers in Robotics and AI*, last modified March 22, 2018, https://www.frontiersin.org/articles/10.3389/frobt.2018.00026/full.